Here I am

Luisella von Schönberg
A fearless life from Baroness to the Gulag and back

by Christina von Ditfurth

Foreword by Jill Wran

As a literary agent I read, and set aside, many unpublished manuscripts but in the case of *Here I am again* I was utterly captivated, compelled to read on and sad to my soul when the saga ended with the death of Luisella. Her story gives new meaning to the expression 'a woman of means'.

Yes, to begin with she was well off financially but the riches which really mattered were a deep resolve to live an independent life close to the land she cherished, a certain resignation to her lot no matter what, and the remarkable energy which she brought to every single living day.
A woman of great, if petite presence, Luisella is in many respects a model for women everywhere today.

But I see three other heroines in *Here I am again*.
First, Luisella's mother Emma, who also turned away from a privileged life for the charm of her husband's wild estate, and indeed died for it. Secondly, Christina for piecing together the stories of these two magnificent women and bringing her own charm and inimitable spirit to the task.
Finally, and not least, there is Christina's own mother, Maria, who by befriending Luisella made Christina's work possible.

Love, freedom, tragedy and captivity.
This is not just the story of another intrepid lady exhumed for posterity but that of women of significance whose very lives embodied European history during an extended period of momentous upheaval.

Dedication by Christina von Ditfurth

This book is for my mother, Maria, who never ceased to be fascinated by Luisella, her mother-in-law.

She urged me to write a book about Luisella's unusual life. I agreed, and subsequently, my mother spent hours recording the family history and memories of Luisella on tape, in German, which my cousin Lolo, a skilled typist, kindly transcribed. With the transcript at hand, I kept unlocking secrets and filling gaps by asking my mother many questions during my regular summer holidays back home in Austria.

The promise to write Luisella's story took a lot longer than I had expected. I have to thank all my friends who patiently kept reading yet another rewritten manuscript and kept encouraging me not to give up.

My special thanks to Karen Kleppich and Andrea Mathews, who wrote the original English translation, which allowed me to complete it in my own style and thanks also to Thérèse Tobin who finessed it.

I thank my husband for the title over which I agonised for years, and Philip von Schönberg and Peggy Eather, for organising the photography of Luisella's portrait for the cover.

It was inspirational to work with my friend Helen Hayes who finally made it all happen and with Trish Maganja who produced the artwork. I am most grateful to both ladies.

*The crest of the
von Schönberg family.*

*The crest of the
von Ditfurth family.*

ANNA CONSTANTIA COUNTESS VON COSEL
AND THE SCHÖNBERG CONNECTION

Anna Constantia
Countess von Cosel 1680-1765

King Augustus II of Poland,
Elector of Saxony 1670-1733

Frederike Alexandrine
1709-1784
m1730
Ian Kanty Count
Moszynskil

Frederick Augustus
Count von Cosel 1712-1770
m1749
Friederike Countess
von Holtzendorff

Augusta Constantia
1708-1728
m1725
Heinrich Friedrich
Count von Friesen

Charlotte Louise
Countess von Cosel 1757-1831
m1781
Rudolf Count von Bünau 1750-1806

Henriette Charlotte Countess
von Bünau 1784-1812
m1807
Frederick Augustus
Wolf von Schönberg 1780-1830

Wolf Erich von Schönberg 1812-1883
m1854
Luisella von Kiel 1833-1857

Erich Donald von Schönberg 1854-1926
m1885
Emma von Osterrieth 1862-1928

Wolf Erich von Schönberg 1895-1981
m1922
Auguste Senft von Pilsach 1897-1989

Luisella von Schönberg 1888-1970
m1911
Moriz Baron von Ditfurth 1873-1935
m1939
George Wilhelm Sacher 1913-1944 (?)

© Christina von Ditfurth 2021
ISBN 978-0-6451578-0-2
Edited by Helen Hayes Media
Design & layout by Trish Maganja

Contents

Preface 8
August 1955 10
A train arrives 16
Where is Tenneck? 20
My memories 26
Čonak becomes part of our family 32
Back to nature 40
Motherly love 47
Just get married quickly 55
World War I 1914-1918 62
My father 68
The reign of terror 74
A day in Čonak 82
A deadly encounter 87
Frau Luisella Sacher 91
Čonak became elegant 98
The Russians are coming 105
The first sign of life 110
Anna Constantia, Countess von Cosel 114
From Baroness to slave 120
Diogenes in the barrel 125
Captured and frustrated 130
Revenge is sweet 140
Dr Ottillinger and the Baroness 146
Life in the Gulag 150
The intimate version 158
In my grandmother's footsteps 161
In Čonak at last 168
Lungau 179
Death 186
Epilogue: Uninvolved and yet familiar! 189
Notes, Footnotes and Photos 192

Preface

*The wolf dies and leaves behind his coat,
a man but his reputation*

❋

"WAR IS THE FATHER OF ALL THINGS," was my Austrian father's favourite saying. He viewed the cruelty of war in a philosophical way: everything gets destroyed, just to be rebuilt again. My father came from a traditional family of soldiers, yet he was never a soldier himself.

I want to capture the story about how both World Wars have affected our fate, how our lives were characterised by our inherited genes, and how our upbringing and times have taken many sudden sharp turns.

Described in this book is my fearless grandmother, revealing her courageous, passionate and unconventional life, her stubbornness, how she took destiny into her own hands and how she had to pay for it with 10 years behind the Iron Curtain in the Soviet Union.

I am a child of war. For many years I have been haunted by nightmares; the air raids during the last days of World War II had a profound effect on my childhood and memories remain even now. Every time I heard thunder and lightning I would escape into my parents' warm bed. To this day, I still don't like watching war movies or war documentaries.

However, when the American occupying forces came charging down the narrow street through our village, in endless military convoys, I found it exciting. We children discovered chewing gum and chocolates; treats given to us by the Americans. I admired the fashionable officers' wives who brought a touch of elegance into our grey existence after the War, where any kind of luxury had been unknown to us.

The signing of the Austrian State Treaty in 1955, which liberated Austria from all occupying forces and granted her independence and neutrality, was a milestone in our lives. For my age group, World War II had not yet been included in our history lessons; the burden of reality was still too raw. Only one generation later, the War had become a subject one could talk about.

The War had a lasting effect on my family. My young parents were forced to move from their home in Vienna to various provincial towns in Austria. They ended up in a small village surrounded by mountains in the state of Salzburg – mountains that played a big part in my future. We escaped hunger, then we fled the Russians. In between, we played cat and mouse with the Nazis and at the very last moment slipped through the deadly grasp of communism.

After 12 years living in Tenneck, my family moved back to a totally changed Vienna. Good luck and bad luck had their very own dynamic interplay.

Nothing would ever be the same again.

Christina Ditfurth, August 2021

NB. The aphorisms in this book are taken from the booklet *Chinese Wisdoms and Stories* (Scheuermann-Verlag, Vienna), which my mother gave to my father for Christmas in 1949.

August 1955

*The world is an ocean,
our hearts are its shores*

❁

Even though it was one of those last few hot days of summer, my father froze. He had not heard of his mother for years.

Here in Tenneck, in our enclosed valley surrounded by mountains, we were thankful for every ray of sunshine. I was 12 years old and shared a room with my brother Nikolaus, who is two years older than me. Our room was quite spacious, but still small enough to throw a pillow across at my brother's bed. Our black cat could jump in one giant leap from the door onto one of our beds – although bouncing competitions on our beds were strictly forbidden. The room had a large window, which looked down the main street of town. My mother's much-loved piano also found a place in our room. It was only small, so there wouldn't have been room for a grand piano.

It was then that I experienced my first sleepless night, tossing and turning restlessly from side to side. In the darkness, my eyes searched over and over for the imposing oil painting of my grandmother, hanging in a thick black wooden frame above our beds.

My whole fascination was with her jewellery: the perfect single-strand pearl necklace with a glittering diamond clasp, her pearl earrings with small diamonds and the magnificent diamond brooch, which sat on her lightly-coloured silk blouse, deep on her décolletage, sparkling even in the dark. This is exactly how I imagined an elegant, sophisticated lady. The lush, dark and fashionably arranged hair matched her full eyebrows, and her melancholic eyes looked longingly into the distance. That's when I thought: that's her – my grandmother.

Tenneck in the state of Salzburg, Austria.

I kept wondering – do we look alike? I have her dark eyebrows. I also have blue-grey eyes, but I have light blonde hair. I was too young and impatient to dwell on further differences.

Tomorrow I will meet her for the first time in my life. She will be arriving by express train from Vienna in the afternoon.

In excited anticipation of her arrival, my brother wasn't sleeping well either. Never before had we talked so much about my grandmother as that night; our imaginations ran wild. What would she look like now? What stories would she tell us?

When we were old enough to read and write, we noticed that our father, whenever he wrote his mother's name, added a cross to it. Sometimes we would ask him, "Do you really think she is dead?" He always replied with a laconic "Yes." Our mother, however, would always say "No," or "We don't know." Any further questions we asked about our grandmother mostly received a single word reply from our parents, and since we didn't know her, our curiosity was easily satisfied. So, no further questions were asked.

Actually, my parents had not heard from her for six years, since the spring of 1949. Before then we had often received weekly letters from her. But the last two letters my mother had sent to her had come back with a Russian stamp saying *'retour – parti'*. My grandmother had simply vanished behind the Iron Curtain without a trace. Anything could have happened.

Probably she had fallen ill and died – although in her last letter she had not complained of being ill. She could have been assassinated – she did have enemies. Had she been run over by a lorry and died at the roadside, bleeding to death? All our theories were pure speculation.

After all, about 60 million people had died by the end of World War II, so the cross by my grandmother's name could have been justified. On the other hand, there was no official death notice, so it could have been that she was just one of the huge number of people still missing. Since 1945 the German government had efficiently created 53 million files containing the fate of about 30 million missing persons. Luckily, it was about that time that the first computers were built. They were huge, slow machines.

As my parents struggled to survive, our missing grandmother faded into the background for the time being. We were lucky, our family was still complete: father, mother, son and daughter. My father was never called up to serve in the army. He was a Hungarian citizen living in Austria, which meant that neither Hitler, who annexed Austria, nor the Hungarians were able to conscript him.

Two years after grandmother's disappearance, in the spring of 1951, my mother was able to visit Vienna for the first time since the War. The city had by then been divided into four administrative zones by the American, French, English and Russian allied occupation forces. It was not only Vienna that had been divided into four zones but the whole of Austria. We were lucky that our little village fell into the American zone.

The train journey to Vienna was almost like travelling overseas. My mother had to have an identity pass written in four languages (German, English, Russian and French) validated by 11 official stamps.

At Enns River, which is roughly in the middle of Austria, my mother crossed the demarcation line, where she had to undergo a full body search. Could her unconventional hairstyle have aroused suspicions? My mother was very modern for her time; she had a fashionable 'Eton haircut', a very short, slicked-down version of the crop, worn by both men and women since the early 1920s. Back on the train, she proceeded with an uncomfortable feeling towards the Russian Zone of Vienna.

Nowhere else in Austria could she look through an official Red Cross list for missing persons. But under what name would my grandmother appear on the endless lists?

Option one: her maiden name, Luisella von Schönberg, which could be written with or without the 'von', as in Germany the aristocratic title remained part of the name even after the War.

Option two: Luisella Ditfurth, this time without the 'von', as in Austria all aristocratic titles had been abolished. In this case, she would have chosen the name of her late husband, the name of her only child, my father. As there's only one Ditfurth family in Austria, it would have been a logical choice.

Option three: Luisella Sacher, the name of her second husband, for whom she had turned her back on Austria and gone to spend the rest of her life with him in Čonak, in the Carpathian Mountains.

Which criteria would she have chosen in her choice of name: logic or emotion?

My mother had no option but to spend hours checking all three names, in a variety of spellings, but no resemblance to the name of Luisella Schönberg, Ditfurth or Sacher was to be spotted. The thought that she must be dead went through her mind again.

As a last resort, she went to the Russian Commandant's Office at Palais Epstein and filed a request for investigation. That's all she could do.

And so, my father's theory that my grandmother was dead gained more and more credibility with each successive year. I found it somehow exciting that we had a grandmother but that we did not know if she was alive or dead. For me, she was rather like a ghost.

Whenever she was mentioned in a conversation, which rarely occurred in front of us children, nothing good was said about her.

My father, who had nicknames for everyone, only talked of my grandmother as *Die Alte* (the Old Woman), her official nickname, with which she herself signed her letters to my parents. However, my grandmother's preferred family nickname was *Die Uralhexe* (the Witch of the Urals), a strong and frightening nickname which painted a negative image of her for us children. Somehow the name *Uralhexe* did not fit with the dignified portrait in our room. Why would they call her a witch? I didn't know if I should be pleased or scared to meet this grandmother of mine. The oil painting portrayed my grandmother in her youth and I did not imagine that in the meantime she had become an old woman.

But tomorrow she would arrive as a 67-year-old refugee, returning home after being held captive in a Russian labour camp for six years.

In this hot summer of 1955, we went on our furthest vacation so far in our new Jeep. Our journey took us from Tenneck through Scandinavia all the way to Finland. We all enjoyed travelling and especially car journeys. In the years after the war, hardly any *Autobahnen* (motorways) existed and my brother and I sat with our faces glued to the car windows, looking curiously at the unknown landscape. To save money during our journey, we often shared a room with our parents. I found it so thrilling that all four of us were sleeping in one room – it was my idea of family fun.

And then, during this happy and untroubled holiday, a postcard from our 'dead' grandmother was included amongst my father's forwarded work mail. It was as if lightning had struck: the holiday was ruined, said my mother. He had erased *Die Alte* with a certain relief from his life years ago – now she was back.

My grandmother wrote:

"My dear Franzl.
I am on my way to you, my loved ones, and I am very excited to see you all. I am very well. I don't know just yet when I will be arriving in Tenneck – probably around the end of August or beginning of September. Could you please send me a parcel via the Red Cross, as everyone here receives parcels. I desperately need something for my feet, like some plain tennis shoes, something I can wear around the camp.
The camp shoes here are so heavy. I have money to buy some things, but there is nothing to buy here. Also, sugar and coffee and anything to smear on a piece of bread would be appreciated. My shoe size is 38.
Hugs to the children. What will they think of their grandmother?
Looking forward to seeing you soon and a big group hug to you all.
Kiss, Die <u>Alte</u>."

Alte was underlined. (I saw this postcard for the first time when I was reading through my grandmother's correspondence to research this book.)

And now the moment had finally arrived. "What shall I wear today" was a very important question because I wanted to make a good first impression on my grandmother. There was not much to choose from, as most of my clothes were hand-me-downs from other children. Because we were living in the American occupied zone, we sometimes had access to special things, like nylon fabrics.

For this special occasion, I chose my favorite bolero dress, which my mother had made for me on her Singer sewing machine, in a light-blue nylon fabric with yellow daisies. As I looked at myself with excitement in the mirror, I glanced at my brown shoes, hand-me-downs from my brother; staring right back at me, they were so chunky and didn't go with the dress. But we had no money for new shoes. We were lucky to have any shoes at all.

After that sleepless night, I wrestled into my dress – no luxury of a zip. Wearing that dress, which I still remember to this day, I felt like a young lady, ready to meet my 'new' grandmother.

The road to Werfen.

A train arrives

Returning home is often harder than leaving

❋

Tenneck, with its population of only 500, was not important enough to be a fast-train stop, so we had to drive three kilometres to the next town of Werfen, where the fast trains did stop. Our daily commute to the elementary school in Werfen took us along the same route, so we knew every stretch of this narrow, winding road along the Salzach river. On this particular day, the three kilometres seemed to take a lot longer.

My brother and I had picked some wildflowers, which we tied together with a red ribbon. In the car we practiced presenting the flowers with our left hand, so we could kiss our grandmother's right hand. My sweaty hands nearly crushed the flowers.

My heart was pounding heavily as the train from Vienna pulled into the station, right on time. We stared intensely and in silence at each opening coach door. Then, towards the back of the train, we saw a small white-haired woman in a black dress and a heavy black quilted jacket, with a bundle thrown over her shoulder, jump down from the high steps of the train onto the platform. This first impression of energy and vitality was something only my parents understood. Together as a family, we walked towards her, but none of us had the urge to run. I later found out that in all those lonely years she had dreamt that we children would run towards her, into her open arms. But why would we? She was a complete stranger to us, with a scary nickname.

Her blue-grey eyes sparkled, and with her mouth half open she mumbled, "Here I am again." Without any emotion, my father replied, "Yes, here you are again." As was expected of him, he kissed her hand formally and took the bundle off her shoulders. My mother gave her a hug, and we children gave her our flowers and kissed her hand, just as we had rehearsed. With that, the welcome was over with no tears and no fuss.

I was sorely disappointed. She had short, snow-white hair and not a tooth in her mouth. With her wrinkled face, she looked like a Russian peasant. Nothing like the beautiful lady in the portrait hanging above our beds.

We hopped into our Jeep and drove back to Tenneck. In our family, children only spoke when we were spoken to, so I looked curiously at my grandmother, who was sitting in the front seat of the car and listened. My mother engaged in lively conversation with her, while my father concentrated on driving. Even worse than her looks, was the shock of hearing her very strong German accent. We speak German in Austria but have a much softer pronunciation and rhythm to the language – similar to the difference in English between the Scottish accent and the English accent. Her German was perfect and although she had certainly not forgotten the language, using the words *mal* for *einmal* (once) or *nee* for *nein* (no) at least once in every sentence added to the 'Germanic feeling'.

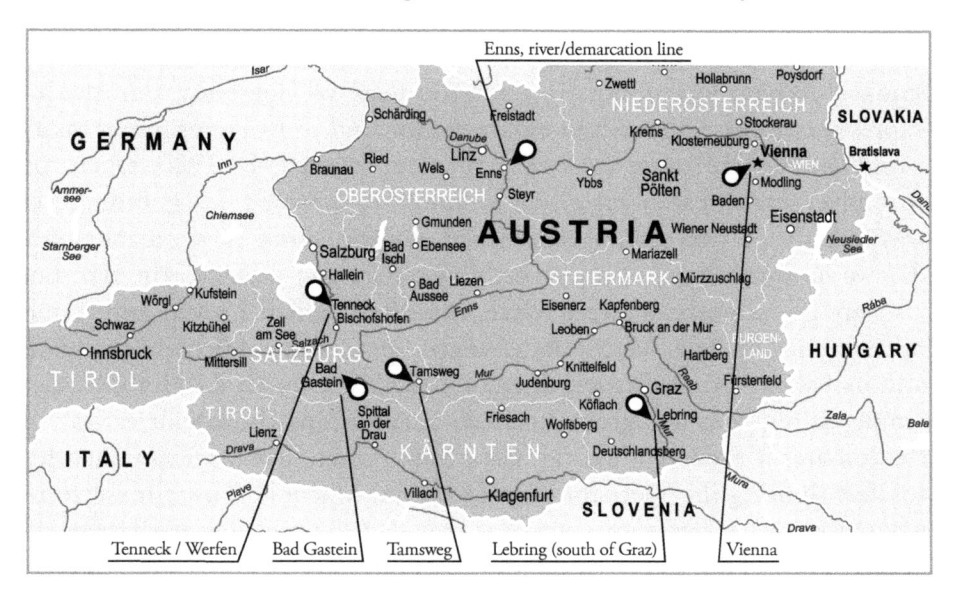

Our grandmother moved into the back room, adjacent to the bedroom I shared with my brother. This meant she had to walk through our space to get to the only lavatory in our flat. Up to now, this area had been the maid's bedroom. Before, during and after the War we always had servants, because so many people were made homeless and were willing to work for board and lodging. Our last maid was Hungarian and was getting too old to cope with all the tricks we played on her. When the time was right for her to move out, our grandmother arrived and moved in. From then on, we also shared the only bathroom with her, which she used with great consideration and always kept tidy.

We sat in our small living room with our 'new' long-lost grandmother as she unpacked her *Pinkerl* (bundle) of possessions. To our great surprise, she pulled out three tins of caviar, a bottle of vodka and some tea – a farewell gift to her from 'Official Russia'.

Of course, we children had never heard of caviar; I seem to remember that we didn't like it, but our parents were very excited – Russian caviar was considered to be one of the finest caviars in the world. She showed off her other treasures: a tin spoon, with which she had eaten during her captivity, a pair of scissors, which another camp inmate had made for her, and some Machorka, a sweet-smelling strong tobacco also known as peasant tobacco. Another most treasured item was her second pair of reading glasses, which she had had to smuggle in and out of various camps, as it was forbidden to own two pairs of reading glasses. "*Nee*, I wasn't afraid, I hid them well," she told us. She was truly born fearless, with no end of courage.

From then on, the atmosphere and the smell in our apartment, on the second floor of the office building of the *Eisenwerk* (Iron Works) *Sulzau-Werfen,* changed. Throughout her life my grandmother was a heavy smoker. Maybe it was not only for the taste of cigarettes, but also to express her independence and emancipation and to fit better into a man's world, because in those days all 'real men' smoked. In 1926, when the first advertisement showing a woman smoking appeared, my grandmother was already 38 and a long-established smoker. From now on, not only did we have the smell of my father's cigarettes and cigars in the flat, but also my grandmother's sweet Machorka smell, which I loved and found rather a nice change. Machorka *(Nicotina rustica)* is a wild tobacco plant and native to warm subtropical regions, but it can easily survive in cooler temperatures, as it was grown in fields surrounding the labour camp. To the inmates it probably had the same importance that marijuana had for soldiers fighting the Vietnam War. However, Machorka, usually rolled in newspaper, was a harmless drug that provided the prisoners with a feeling of pleasure and a whiff of luxury.

My grandmother insisted that Machorka rolled in the Russian *Pravda* newspaper tasted a lot better than rolled in the Austrian *Presse*. In the labour camp she could never finish reading the *Pravda*, as it was immediately seized for rolling cigarettes. When her Machorka stash came to an end, she was truly sad and changed unhappily to cigarettes without filters. To save money, she always smoked the cheapest sort. If there was one thing she missed about Russia, it would be Machorka.

My grandmother, Luisella.

Where is Tenneck?

*Half an orange is just
as sweet as a whole one*

❋

People look quite astonished when I say, "I am from Tenneck." Nobody has ever heard of the place. Tenneck is squeezed between two mountain ranges, a river and a main road. The centre of town is still the *Eisenwerk Sulzau-Werfen,* the hub of all life in and around Tenneck. Salzburg, the principal town in the district is about 40 kilometres away. The region has a long history. Thanks to the iron ore deposits in the nearby mountains, the *Eisenwerk Sulzau-Werfe*n became the first blast furnace and hammer mill, opening in 1770. At that time, the Catholic Church had power over all walks of life within the Austrian Empire and it was the Archbishop of Salzburg who founded this first blast furnace, which produced simple cast-iron pieces such as chimney plates. By 1850, the technology was already so well developed that it produced technically advanced iron parts which could be exported all over Europe.

The iron ore deposits were exhausted in 1960 and the blast furnace operations ceased. However, the high-tech induction furnaces continue to produce top quality work rolls (for shaping steel), which are now sold worldwide. The specialised technology of the iron works has gained an international reputation and it provides for hundreds of families in the area. The Weinberger family bought the iron foundry more than 100 years ago, and with over 240 years of work experience, it is still one of the most lucrative private companies in the state of Salzburg.

Our friendship with the Weinberger family began through a common passion: Emil Weinberger was as keen a hunter as my father was. As young students in Vienna, they would spend their holidays hunting deer, wild boar, bears, foxes and anything that crawled or flew in the virgin forests of my grandmother's estate in the Carpathian Mountains, which was within a day's drive of Vienna.

Although my father had a degree in agriculture, he became the Company Secretary of the iron works in 1945, at the end of World War II, when Austria was occupied. He had a good knowledge of English, so he worked for Emil's brother Rolf (who couldn't speak English) and established the necessary contacts with the American Occupation Force.

Approximately 70,000 American soldiers were stationed in Austria during the autumn of 1945. Tenneck played a significant role during this time, as the private road to Blühnbach Castle branched off from here. The Americans called it *Blumback* and the 80-room castle was used as a relaxation retreat for its officers. The Krupp family, the former owners and friends of my parents, had to vacate the castle but were allowed to live in the grounds in a modest house. The Americans loved the pomp and glamour of the castle; maybe they felt they were living in a sort of Disneyland. There were no orgies of destruction; on the contrary, they admired and appreciated the elegance of the place and lit all the beautiful chandeliers day and night.

Rolf and Marie-Louise Weinberger welcomed my family as refugees with open arms. Nowadays it is hard to imagine, but our two families shared a common household and lived together in an apartment in the company's administration building for four years. You might think that two women in the kitchen together would be trouble, that it couldn't work. However, my mother never had any interest in

The Amtshaus – our home in Tenneck.

cooking and kitchen duties, while Marie-Louise was an excellent cook, so our life worked out wonderfully well. All of us children were of a similar age and we had a fantastic time growing up together.

For us young girls, the American officers' wives with their dyed blonde hair and their perfect white teeth seemed the most elegant women in the world! We would often sit on a pile of gravel on the road leading to Blühnbach waiting for them to pass by in their open Jeeps, just to get a glimpse of the height of glamour in this world.

After four years of communal living, the Weinberger family moved to the Windbichl estate, and we had the whole apartment to ourselves. This meant that from now on I had to walk up a steep hill to play with the Weinberger children. But the trek was always worthwhile: it was really exciting and good fun at Windbichl. They had a great barnyard with chickens, pigs, cows and horses. Once I was even allowed to milk a cow! My daily job was to fetch milk from Windbichl. One day some American soldiers made fun of me as I was making my way back from there with two full cans of milk, walking on the narrow pavement; they drove up close behind me, all of a sudden loudly hooting their horns, which gave me such a fright that I dropped both cans of milk. They laughed out of the windows, waving at me, and drove on. I continued home in tears and with no milk.

We had a small garden on one side of the administration building, where a huge chestnut tree majestically claimed its place. Our annual autumn ritual was to collect chestnuts, roast them and then devour them.

During the wintertime, the snow would turn blackish very quickly, because we were living so close to the iron works. But that concerned us very little; we would still make snowmen with a real carrot for a nose and build igloos which we furnished with old rugs and where we lit candles – all quite an adventure for us children. We also had a large concrete area, which wasn't that attractive but rather practical. During the summer months when the works were closed at the weekend, we could go wild on our roller skates and try out some stunts with our bikes.

As in every small town, we had a *Gasthaus* in Tenneck; it was called Gasthaus Brunner. We also had a bakery and a small corner shop; there was no school or church, but our town had a public swimming pool, which had wood-panelled walls. Our mother, who was a champion swimmer, taught us, along with half the village, the crawl (freestyle), breast and backstroke.

*With the Weinberger children and our nannies in Tenneck.
I am second from right and my brother is wearing the beanie.*

On particularly hot days, the women officers from Blühnbach came to the pool and cooled down with us. Oh, how I envied them when I saw their colourful, ruffled nylon bikinis. I felt so miserable in my Bordeaux-coloured crochet swimwear, which my mother had made for me. I dreamt of growing up and getting out into the big wide world.

However, I was proud to live in the yellow building with green shutters, the most beautiful building in the village. In Tenneck, everyone greeted everyone in the streets. As our village was only small and there were too few children, we had to travel three kilometres to the elementary school in Werfen. The iron works provided a bus for the school children in the morning but coming home often meant walking along the dangerously narrow road with no pavement.

Since my parents had grown up in Vienna and had no experience of life in the mountains, they needed to adjust to a totally different lifestyle, which they embraced with gusto. Come sun, rain or snow, every weekend we went hiking in the summer and skiing in the winter. With the exhortation, "Come on, you are not made of sugar," the alarm would ring mercilessly at 6.30am, even on Sundays. Our weekday breakfast, *Buttersemmel* (buttered bread roll) with apricot jam, was accompanied by a soft-boiled egg as a bonus, before we headed off into the mountains.

My mother became the best berry collector of all time. In the surrounding forests we would still find wild strawberries, raspberries and blueberries in abundance. Wild mushrooms also hugely enhanced our otherwise bland diet.

Because I had to keep up with my older brother, I learned to ski at the age of three. In winter we hiked up the hill with our 'wooden planks' and then raced each other downhill, hoping to make it without falling over. The Weinberger children were our constant companions. We also sledged down the forest trails and if there was a frozen pond somewhere, we would go ice skating and try pirouettes with our borrowed skates.

We had no ski lifts in Tenneck, so every Sunday (Saturday was still a working day and we had school) we drove to one of the nearby ski resorts with a ski lift. We often went to Radstadt and Obertauern, and on the long and slow ascents by chairlift, I would watch the technique of other skiers. My parents had no money for luxuries such as hiring a ski instructor. However, one day an instructor who had been watching me and thought I had talent got me started at ski racing. At the age of 17 I became a member of the Austrian National Ski Racing Team, and so my life took off in a whole new direction.

My dream of seeing the world beyond the mountains of Tenneck started to take shape.

*From top:
My first race; even a broken leg didn't stop me; with Canadian skiing legend, Nancy Greene (right).*

My memories

It is of human nature to talk little

※

My grandmother, *Die Alte, Die Uralhexe*, adapted very quickly to our life in Tenneck. And the atmosphere at home changed. Our table manners were watched more strictly at dinner. We rarely had the courage to ask our grandmother anything, or to speak without being asked first. Unlike my other grandmother, *Die Alte* was not a 'cuddly' grandmother who greeted us with a broad smile and open arms. Wary of this stranger with the foreign accent, we were too intimidated to dare to sit on her lap. Actually, it never occurred to us to do so. Perhaps she longed for it but could never show it. Formality always had the upper hand; emotions and affections were buried deep. Whenever she frowned and looked angry, I stole quietly out of the room.

Despite the sharp hook nose, which would have been better suited to a man's face, it was her piercing eyes that dominated her every expression. Over the years her eyes had sunk deep into her face, yet they had a sharpness to them, unlike the longing gaze portrayed in the oil painting. She would stare at you intensely during every conversation. At just 12 years of age, I was as tall as my grandmother, and I was glad to have inherited my mother's figure. My grandmother was stocky with very short strong legs and chunky hands. I can't describe her in a more flattering way because it wouldn't be the truth. But her energy and vitality matched her appearance, and her manly handshake confirmed her strength. Although she was 67 years old and had snow-white hair, with her quick walk, upright posture and deep voice, she never gave in to thoughts of 'being old' or 'feeling sorry for herself'. In her emotional world, there was no room for whining or crying. She would have found sentiments such as "Oh, that poor woman," or "My dear God, what you have been through!" simply ridiculous. She didn't want pity but demanded respect and recognition from everybody she met. Thank goodness for her great sense of humour, though, which would make her laugh out loud wholeheartedly and her sternness would just vanish for a little while.

I started to like my grandmother much more once she had her new set of teeth. Also, her new haircut with a blueish rinse gave her a more feminine touch. The brown age spots on her hands were covered with a spot concealer. That surprised me and showed a level of vanity that I did not expect.

During the first few weeks, my grandmother would only eat with her tin spoon and she would not touch our silver cutlery. As we very rarely had meat for dinner, this wasn't a problem and I was fascinated by how deftly she ate with her spoon. Slowly she got used to using a knife and fork again. She continued to hide the few items she had brought from her old life in captivity under her pillow and some under her mattress. When we asked her about it, she replied, "*Ach,* it's just a habit I am used to, because in the labour camp I had to hide everything." And that was the end of the topic. So, the precious second pair of reading glasses was placed carefully under her pillow every night. It took a few weeks before she'd leave possessions such as reading glasses, book, Machorka and a lighter lying around openly in her room.

Her daily ritual, after breakfast, was to read the newspaper. My grandmother had a great interest in the new political situation in Austria. She soaked up world events and information like a sponge and she never missed the news on the radio either. The BBC was her favourite station. Her English was still impeccable. She loved discussions – or rather, she insisted that her opinion was heard.

Initially she still drank very strong black tea, about which my father always liked to comment, "The spoon gets stuck in your teacup", because she scooped countless spoons of sugar into her tea. "*Ach, Kindchen* (child), this was my elixir of life, which gave me energy," because, as she would tell us later, "We only got 27 grams of sugar per person per day in the labour camp. I often gave away my sugar ration to the poor people outside the camp who came begging at the barbed-wire fence as they had less to eat than us."

From the beginning, my grandmother showed much more interest in my brother than in me. This was partly because he was the grandson and only heir, and partly because she loved men much more than women.

Wherever there was an empty chair next to a man and one next to a woman, she would always choose to sit next to the man. At cocktail parties she would always stand in a group of men. With my brother she wanted to talk, wanted to pick him up from school and wanted to form a bond. But as a 14-year-old teenager going through puberty, he wasn't really open to anyone, let alone his grandmother. For him she was still the 'Witch of the Urals', and to any questions she had for him, he would give a short and abrupt reply.

Whenever my grandmother entered our little sitting room, my father, sitting comfortably in his favourite chair, would exchange a few meaningless words with her, and then quickly disappear behind his newspaper. It was obvious that he was ignoring her presence and didn't want his everyday life to be interrupted. Did she think, "Oh, that's just how Franzl is?" And was she satisfied with that? Or did it enter her head that her only child, her son, had written off his mother.

At dinnertime we hardly ever talked about her past decade in Russia. Usually there was a lot of 'social gossip', but daily life with its own little problems was the focus now. For my grandmother, the 'Russian chapter' was closed, as she looked to the future ahead of her. And it wasn't her son, Franzl, who looked after her and drove her around, but rather her daughter-in-law, Maria. The dentist's appointment came first. My mother drove her to Bischofshofen, to the nearest dentist. To make the 20-kilometre round trip worthwhile, my grandmother decided to have the roots of her 16 lost teeth taken out in one go! "*Nee*, it wasn't fun, but such pain is quickly over." She couldn't wait to be able to chew properly again. After that, we had more delicious dinners at home, rather than spinach, soups and porridge.

And to go with her bright new white teeth, she also got new clothes. My mother took her to Salzburg. She chose a dark green, finely patterned shirtwaist silk dress – a dress with a flowery pattern and ruffles wouldn't have suited her at all. She also got some practical leather shoes – and she almost looked like a lady again. There was only one thing missing: PEARLS! My mother remembered her favourite saying: "If a woman has nothing at all, it does not matter – but pearls in her ears are a must." They went shopping for pearls.

With the start of a new school year, serious life began again for us. And we had gotten used to having my grandmother in the room next to us.

This is the point where I want to tell you that my grandmother, together with her younger brother, Wolf, owned a property in the Carpathian Mountains (today in the Ukraine), called Čonak. My brother and I had been familiar with the name Čonak since we were born. It had not taken long for Uncle Wolf, her brother, to realise that Čonak was too small for 'two heads' and since he had to look after the estates in Saxony, it hadn't been too difficult for him to leave the management of Čonak in his sister's hands. Letter writing was one of the hobbies the siblings had enjoyed, and the correspondence between them had always been rather lively; they liked to criticise one another and insisted that their own opinion was clearly set out and heard. Family gossip was also important. But this had all ended very abruptly in 1949. No more letters had arrived from Čonak. Independently from my parents, who only had very loose contact with Uncle Wolf, he also believed that his sister must have died.

As soon as the time was right, meaning as soon as my grandmother had her new set of teeth and was ready to meet people, our Uncle Wolf and his wife Gusti came to visit. They came all the way from Tegernsee in Germany, where he and his family had put down new roots at the end of

The main house at Čonak that became such a part of our family history.

the War. In those days this was a full day's journey. He rented a minibus, so he could bring a surprise for his sister: two Sudeten German couples who were employed to oversee the hunting in Čonak and consequently had become, over many years, part of the family. Uncle Wolf had organised their timely escape from Čonak before Russia had occupied the area and closed the borders. After their successful escape and arrival in Germany, he had considered it his duty and social responsibility to help them find employment, which he duly did through relatives in Bavaria. So, this small group arrived in Tenneck and installed itself in the Gasthaus Brunner. Uncle Wolf brought a bottle of French champagne to celebrate his reunion with his sister in style. This was a very noble gesture! My grandmother had kept back a tin of Russian caviar. My mother thoroughly enjoyed this taste of luxury, and for days afterwards she would tell us how delicious the caviar with champagne was.

Uncle Wolf was a small, formal man who liked to be taken seriously. As the head of the family von Schönberg, a noble German family, he saw it as his duty and responsibility to assert his influence in all areas of the family. Traits such as social awareness, correctness, diligence and a passion for meddling in other people's lives, he shared with his sister. For example, as my father was his only nephew, his upbringing and education were very important to Uncle Wolf. He often commented on my father's bad manners. This angered his sister very much: what could her brother, seven years younger than her, know about bringing up children? She protected her son unconditionally because "It was none of his business, and what impudence." Such criticism weakened the sibling love a little.

As our apartment was too small for such an invasion of visitors and we didn't have enough plates and chairs for a family dinner on that scale, we had the Gasthaus Brunner set up a separate room for our guests. We children, although we were 12 and 14 years old, were still treated like little children and therefore weren't invited to the family reunion. As we so often did, we ate with Steffi, our cook, in the kitchen.

Years later my mother told me that after the formal family welcome, at which Uncle Wolf kissed her hand, my grandmother had tears in her eyes when Hermann, the chief hunter at Čonak, hugged her spontaneously. There was not a hint of tension, ill feeling or jealousy, just pure joy and feelings of deep friendship. My grandmother was often more concerned about the welfare of her employees than that of her own family.

At that moment, did my grandmother feel 'silly' because she hadn't escaped to the West in time, like all the others? "No," my mother said when I asked her about it. *Die Alte* had always overestimated herself. She could never admit mistakes and stood by her principal: "I went my own way."

They chatted until the small hours of the morning, with the guest of honour leading the conversation, eagerly recounting her years behind the Iron Curtain and catching up on all the news about the much-loved Čonak.

She repeated what she had hinted at in her letters before her captivity: the rapid destruction of the surrounding nature, the deforestation, the total ruin of agriculture since the country had been occupied by the Russians. This was a topic she had had to treat carefully in her letters for fear of censorship. Within a few years there were no more deer roaming the forests, the chirping of birds had fallen silent, there were no crabs, and no more trout hiding under stones in the rivers.

Only returnees, like her, could bring news about the real situation behind the Iron Curtain. The communist propaganda machine was in full swing, and western media like CNN did not exist in those days. One really didn't know anything at all. Stories about various local families and their fate were awaited with great anticipation, although my grandmother, given that she had spent six years in the labour camp, was no longer up to date on the latest developments in life in and around Čonak.

I am certain that she delivered a very factual report, because as long as it was not about personal matters, she was very objective and had a gift for meticulous observation. That evening she delivered the official version of her time in Russian captivity. No one could guess that there was a second, more intimate version, which my mother, with her finest detective skills, pieced together like a puzzle over the following weeks.

Čonak becomes part of our family

Even a King has poor relations

❋

The Čonak estate lies within the West Carpathian region, which was under Hungarian administration for over 600 years. In various documents, therefore, Čonak was spelt with a 'z': Czonak. After World War I, during the Czechoslovakian administration, Čonak was written with a *hacek* above the C, but the pronunciation stayed the same: 'Tschonak', which means 'narrow boat or barge'. And indeed, visible in the distance, a barge-like hill rises unexpectedly from the fields.

My grandmother and her brother were third-generation owners of the Čonak estate, as it was their grandfather – Wolf Erich von Schönberg – that bought it. He was an attractive man, who, with his dark hair and olive skin, looked more Mediterranean than German, and who had adventure in his blood. At only 25 years of age and after completion of his studies at the *Dreissigacker Academy of Forestry*, he could not be prevented from going on his first big journey with his best friend. He very much embraced the rapid modernisation of the world. By 1834 there was already an established express mail service between Geneva and Paris, which took only three days. This might have been helpful for the two young men to contact friends and relatives en route and organise some accommodation before they set off for Paris in 1837. With horses, carriages, guns and other assorted luggage, they continued their travels through Italy to Jerusalem and all the way to Egypt. Wolf Erich had a lifelong fascination with Asia Minor, which we now call the Middle East. Time and again over the course of his life, he would travel back there. What fuelled his passion? The mysterious unknown, people speaking in foreign languages, its religion or its history and culture?

However, in his first year of travel and much to his great sorrow, he had to cut short his stay unexpectedly and return to his father's deathbed in Saxony. With his last few breaths, his father urged him not to sell Herzogswalde, the family estate, to his brother but rather to stay and manage it himself. In vain did his father try to tie his adventurous, globetrotting son to the German soil forever.

Despite his inheritance, Wolf Erich – now 28 years old – couldn't bring himself to stay, and in 1840, he started packing and saddling up the horses once again. This time India was his destination, but he had to stop in England first, where he visited his college friend Albert, now Prince Consort to Queen Victoria.

There's an amusing anecdote about this visit: having tea with the Queen at Windsor Castle, where Wolf Erich was invited to stay for a while, the two college friends had a conversation in German, which angered the Queen, because she wanted to be included. So, unashamed, she dipped her fingers in her teacup and sprinkled them both with tea: "English please, gentlemen!"

India was still a colony of the British Empire and Queen Victoria was its head. She personally wrote letters of introduction for Wolf Erich's forthcoming journey to India. He could not have wished for anything more useful. I can't help but wonder if those valuable letters were sent with the first stamp, the 'Penny Black', which was issued in Britain in 1840. Or were they dispatched through diplomatic cables, because they didn't trust the new system?

After an eventful and stormy voyage, the British sailing ship was thrown so far off course that it landed unexpectedly at the Cape of Good Hope in the spring of 1841. And now the passionate hunter had arrived in the biggest game paradise of them all. Although Africa was not on his itinerary – Wolf Erich always seems to have been quite flexible – he remained in Africa for nearly a year and hunted all the big game available, fulfilling a hunter's dream. And because Wolf Erich was so enthusiastic about Africa's wildlife, he decided to burn his diary, which contained notes and records of Africa's best wild stocks, to keep some of his shooting-mad compatriots out of this paradise.

Back home, having ticked off the African continent, he became more interested in anthropology than agriculture, and he had still not fulfilled his dream of going to India. So in the summer of 1842, he once again

A painting of Wolf Erich von Schönberg exhibited in the Old Masters Picture Gallery in Dresden.[1]

boarded a British sailing ship, and eventually, after a turbulent voyage, he arrived at his destination – India. In the large port city of Calcutta, he first re-established his 'land legs', before boarding a comfortable steamboat and travelling slowly north up the 2,500km-long river Ganges. The slow, wide, dirty brown Ganges is venerated by the Indian people as a sacred river. Because all life begins and ends in the Ganges, new-born babies are baptised in it and the dead are sent off to their after-life.

Wolf Erich's initial destination was the pilgrimage city of Benares. Thanks to his royal letter of recommendation, he was welcomed with regal honours by the Maharajah of Benares. Enjoying the luxurious hospitality,

Wolf Erich stayed a few months in this city, where the dead are burned on pyres by the riverside to this day. He studied the country and its people, learned the Hindi language, sketched, wrote and took his time preparing his onward journey. An over-generous farewell gift of elephants and horses, along with some staff, was in equal measure embarrassing and welcome. As good manners demanded and his modest personality allowed, he only accepted after numerous protestations, because he knew he could in no way return the favour. However, he secretly hoped that his amusing companionship and wide-ranging conversation at the Maharajah's Palace could be considered some sort of compensation. Furthermore, he made beautiful charcoal drawings of people, animals and nature, which he offered as a token of gratitude and appreciation.

Today his drawings of diverse natives in their traditional costumes with their weapons have a historical value and are displayed at the *Völkerkundemuseum* (Ethnographic Museum) of Dresden.

Fascinated by the country and its people, he continued to travel. His next destination was Hyderabad, where he was once again received with regal honours. The Nizam of Hyderabad (the Maharaja) welcomed him with festive, colourfully decorated elephants. Now at least he could reciprocate with some of the elephants he had received from the previous Maharaja. He had a modest entourage by now and when he received more gifts upon departure, he did not feel quite as bad since he had 'a little something' of his own to give. Despite being embarrassed, he actually welcomed these gifts as they would add to his 'lean court' and make it easier to reciprocate at the next reception. The Maharajahs of India never grasped the idea that Queen Victoria and Prince Albert could have poor friends.

During his journey through the Punjab region, Wolf Erich fell ill with malaria and was too weak to continue. For many months he had to stay in shared quarters but being a very good-natured and modest man who wanted to get to know the ordinary people, he made the most of this unforeseen calamity. To them he seemed a rich man and one can only assume that savvy Indians exploited him whenever they found an opportunity.

He had a gift for languages, so he used that time to improve his language skills in order to better understand the various local dialects. Meanwhile, he had become very familiar with the country and its people. By the spring of 1843, he was finally well enough to continue his journey northwards, where the Nawab (King) of Oudh prepared a magnificent reception in Lucknow. After an appropriately lengthy stay in the region, he accepted an invitation from the Maharajah Scheer Singh in Lahore (Pakistan today) who also opened his palace gates thanks to another letter from Queen Victoria.

Because of his extraordinary language skills and local knowledge, he was awarded the title *Pasha*, which can be interpreted as 'Lord' and this was added to his family name.

Sadly, my family in Austria knew very little about his travels in India. A recent search on the Internet revealed that "The Baron Erich von Schönberg" had written two volumes, in English, and published them in London in 1853[2]. I guess he did not want to brag to his German relatives, so kept most of his travel stories to himself. He lived in two worlds.

However, the story of a hunting experience with the Nizam of Hyderabad, which could easily have turned into a tragedy, has been handed down from generation to generation within our family. Thanks to Wolf Erich's bravery and experience with animals, he was able to fend off the attack of a wounded lion with great skill and super-human effort, which meant he left the scene victorious. A painting of this duel between man and beast hangs in the picture-gallery at the *Zwinger* in Dresden.

In 1846, after four years of absence and neglect of his family estate, he arrived back home in the courtyard of Herzogswalde with a caravan of horses and carts laden with exotic treasures. My grandmother, Luisella, his granddaughter, inherited some of these treasures; my parents were fortunate enough to be able to save most of them unharmed during World War II, and so my brother and I still have some precious keepsakes of Wolf Erich. An impressive oil painting, showing Wolf Erich standing in a black frock coat, framed in a heavy black wooden frame, occupied the most prominent wall space in our small sitting room in Vienna.

On Wolf Erich's return, he was astonished to see how modern Germany had become and that there was already a 5,470km-long rail network in the country, which meant that, from now on, whenever he caught the travel bug, he just needed to board a train.

My mother often said to me, "You have inherited the travel bug from Wolf Erich." Just like him, I travelled with a close friend halfway around the globe, walking in his footsteps. Our journey started in Australia and took the land route from Madras, South India, all the way to Vienna in a

Toyota Land Cruiser. I travelled the same countries as Wolf Erich 130 years and five generations later – but now the world had become very different. Only Benares, the holy city on the river Ganges, seemed to have remained very similar to how Wolf Erich would probably have experienced it. On the banks of the Ganges, we still saw the burning of the dead on pyres, just as was customary hundreds of years ago. Each year millions of pilgrims visit the Ganges to bathe in it once in their lifetime. Not for anything in this world would I have dared to bathe in the Ganges, not even to put my toes into the muddy water! For someone who has a non-Indian background, it is just amazing how the pilgrims bottle the muddy brown water to take back home with them as their holy water. Superstition, religion, tradition, wealth and poverty, it all becomes entangled and functions harmoniously, which made a deep impression on me. But, unlike Wolf Erich's four-year journey, my world trip only took four months. He had the luxury of having unlimited time, or did he just not care about time? Our luxury was not staying with Maharajas but having a car and sleeping bags. We always found safe places to sleep – at police stations in India, in the forests of Afghanistan or at petrol stations in Turkey. I had only one valuable letter of introduction, which was addressed to the Austrian Ambassador in Tehran, where the luxuries of a bed and a bath awaited us. That was our royal reception! We also couldn't resist the oriental treasures, such as rugs, silverware, paintings and all sorts of knickknacks, but our treasures were nowhere near as valuable in quality or quantity as Wolf Erich's.

As soon as Wolf Erich had managed to oversee everything back home and had succeeded in putting some money in his pockets, he was drawn to the next adventure. In the spring of 1851 the Great Exhibition, the first World Expo, took place in London, and he couldn't have found a better reason to visit his friend Albert again. So, without further ado, he was on his way. The two friends roamed together through the Crystal Palace in Hyde Park, where for the first time in the world one million exhibits were put on display for everybody to see. Prince Albert gave an exhilarating opening speech to 25,000 curious people on 1st May, 1851. The Great Exhibition became a sensational success, with over six million visitors from all over the world.

Inspired by his exciting trip to London, Wolf Erich was once again struck by the 'Wanderlust'. Still fascinated by Asia Minor, he prepared the horses and carriages. Or did he take the train?

Old records show that he spent a long time in Bursa, Turkey.

Then, when he was 42 years old, he all of a sudden and completely out of the blue, married Luisella von Kiel in Montreux, Switzerland.

Why Montreux? Why not whisk her off to Asia Minor? Nobody knows, but I could imagine that the mild climate, the newly built hotels and the ease of train travel lured him there. Maybe he was following in the footsteps of Lord Byron, whom he admired greatly and who was a trendsetter and connoisseur who adored Montreux.

Luisella von Kiel was a pretty, petite woman, who died three years after the birth of her child, Donald, in the year 1857. Once again there was a good reason for Wolf Erich to go travelling. Using the excuse that he wanted to forget this terrible stroke of fate, he returned to his beloved Constantinople, by the Black Sea, in the spring of 1858, with the firm intention of buying a property. For whatever constitutional or political reason, he was denied the purchase of a property. Within the family, we still wonder whether he had intended to leave Germany for good.

However, that may be, his decision to acquire a property somewhere in this part of the world was made. Large areas of land in the Carpathian Mountains, which span 1,700 kilometres, belonged mostly to Hungarian landowners, whose only interest was hunting. In those days, estate agents in the modern sense did not exist. It was customary to purchase or exchange or lease estates amongst trusted friends.

Wolf Erich's Hungarian friend, Count Teleki, said to him one day in 1859, "I have this wonderful family estate in the Carpathian Mountains, where wolves, bears, wild boar, deer and all the game you can only dream of, roam freely in untouched nature – that would be something for you." This roused Wolf Erich's interest; he could already imagine himself chasing a roaring stag through the woods, so he wasted no further time on thoughts of money and finances. Sealing the deal with a handshake, and without seeing the 8,000-hectare property, he bought Čonak.

The dice had been rolled. Debt and gambling were also part of Wolf Erich's life.

More than two years went by before he was able to visit his newly acquired property for the first time. He could not have guessed that this spontaneous purchase, made purely for the gentlemanly pleasure of hunting, should bring his then five-year-old son Donald and future generations heartbreak and tragedy.

How often Wolf Erich actually pursued his passion for hunting in Čonak is unknown, though it is likely that he did not make the journey there very often, but rather left Čonak to its own devices. He was captivated by a new passion: love. The now 51-year-old, still restless and driven by adventure, had fallen in love with a 25-year-old English aristocrat. Needless to say, he pursued her and rather ironically spent more time in England than in the Carpathian Mountains.

When the beautiful English lady Christiana Emmeline Fiennes-Lumley married into the Schönberg family, her nine-year-old stepson, Donald, was already a passionate hunter. He had been taught how to handle a gun responsibly. She instilled in him standards of decency and honesty, conforming to rules of 'fair play', which are still maintained in our family today. During the rutting season, hunting fever prevailed over everything else, so it was just as well the young woman was willing to undertake the long journey, follow the men, and live the simple life in Čonak. The 'back to nature' lure had got hold of the new member of the family too.

A view of Čonak.

Back to nature

Tenderness overcomes the hardest obstacle

Ironically, Čonak was also part of my childhood: in our hallway between the kitchen and the bathroom hung a gold-framed map and a panoramic photo (taken by my father), which I passed many times a day. As well as that, I had a life-size bear mounted above my bed, shot by my father, and many little wolf skins sewn together made up the blanket on my bed. Our apartment was full of hunting trophies, such as a beautifully groomed and mounted boar's head, antlers, tusks and grouse feathers – all silent witnesses to Čonak. In addition, there were many stories told over and over at mealtimes, which were exciting for us children and fired our imagination.

Later, as an adult, it was sometimes difficult for me to understand why my father still talked so enthusiastically about Čonak, although he hadn't been there since my birth.

At that time, I had no idea that my great grandmother Emma (who married my great grandfather Donald at 23 years of age) had lost her heart to Čonak – more than to Donald. What dramas this had entailed.

Emma von Osterrieth, the daughter of a wealthy printing business owner, whose Huguenot family had arrived in Frankfurt during the French Revolution, enjoyed every luxury imaginable. Two family fortunes combined when she married Donald von Schönberg in Frankfurt on 18th August, 1885. She was a talented young painter and had studied under Anton Burger, a member of the *Kronberger* artists' colony. Because her career ended abruptly, only two impressive landscape paintings exist, neither of them in the family. What was the reason for the sudden end of her career as an artist? Did she simply lose interest when getting married to

Lord von Schönberg? Did she secretly paint the magnificent scenery and views of Čonak and then destroy them, because being an artist was not respectable? Or did she view painting as a youthful frivolity not fit for a married woman and just put her brushes and paints away?

The Schönbergs were true Saxons – their wealth came from the Saxon silver mines. Donald managed the inherited family estate Herzogswalde, with its agricultural operations in the Meissen district. Two years after his marriage, Donald, then 29, inherited Čonak. His father Wolf Erich, the globetrotter, had owned it for 24 years before he died in Herzogswalde in 1883, aged 71.

Emma, born into luxury, craved a simple, cosy life, and preferred to spend her days in Čonak, in small rooms with fireplaces and simple wooden furniture rather than in the big, cold rooms of the castle in Saxony. She had no interest in society and snobbery. She left her husband, who was physically strong but weak in character, alone in Germany, where he had his hands full looking after his inherited estates. Could it be that the simple lifestyle suited the bohemian soul of a thwarted artist better? Čonak became the compensation.

Effortlessly, she learned the local language of the people, called Ruthenians (a historical name for Ukrainians from the Carpathian Region). The Ruthenians lived in the valleys of the Carpathian Mountains bordering Ukraine and Slovakia, while the so-called Rusnaks lived in the mountain regions. A third group of people, who lived in the pastoral highlands, were called Huzulen. Their common language was known as Little-Russian or Ruthenian or Rusnakisch. In our home we would just refer to them all as *Rusnaken*. These indigenous farmers and workers, steeped in tradition, religion and superstition, rejected all things modern and continued to live in their ancient ways.

I found this passion for Čonak, which was handed down to my father, quite inexplicable. There was no castle, no park or splendid garden, no lake, no breathtaking view of a mountain – just a pristine, natural environment inhabited by wild animals, which cast a spell not only on men with their passion for hunting but also on women in the family.

While browsing through the innumerable photos of Čonak in leather-bound albums, I could tell that from the road you could only see a small elevation, which was surrounded by a row of tall chestnut trees like a castle wall, denying any sight of the property. A steep narrow road with a canopy

My father's panoramic photo of Čonak.

of more trees led to a driveway. Surprisingly, after only two bends you arrived at the top of a plateau which was a large, grassy expanse and gave you the feeling that you were in the mountains breathing fresh, alpine air. A century-old oak tree dominated the majestic scene. Back then, all the houses were deliberately built lower to harmonise with nature; today we would say they were 'ecofriendly' houses.

The main house, a large, one-storey house with a spacious terrace, was built in the sunniest spot in the meadow. The terrace was protected by an overhanging roof so family and friends could enjoy substantial refreshments in the summer, before going out on an evening hunt. A lovingly landscaped garden with native plants and shrubs surrounded the terrace.

Next to the main house was the kitchen building, close enough to not let the food get cold, but far enough away not to have kitchen smells in the main house. Slightly further away was an old barn, where the venison was processed, hung and dried. This barn was later to be used during my grandmother's 'reign' as a makeshift surgery. Then there was a staff house, where the cook and several domestic helpers lived. The administration and management buildings were further away, below the family home and hidden by a small strip of forest, to separate living from working.

Because Emma found going back and forth to the administration building a nuisance, she ordered a row of trees to be felled, creating a forest clearing rather like a corridor, so she could yell her daily orders directly down to the administration building. My father named it *Schreigasse* – the shouting alley.

Somewhere in the vicinity was the master-of-the-hunt's home with a private garden. He was actually one of the most important people there.

A further four homes for the assistant hunters were scattered around the different hunting areas, each with a small farm attached, with a couple of cows, pigs and chickens so that each family could live self-sufficiently. All these buildings were traditionally built of timber.

Six kilometres away, in the middle of the prime hunting grounds, stood the Rikahaus, which was only opened during the summer for the hunting guests. There were some plans to demolish the Rikahaus in order to replace it with a bigger and more modern building. World War I put an end to these plans and after World War II this part of the property was declared a prohibited area and was surrounded by secrecy. Nobody would offer any information, and when questions were asked, everyone just shrugged their shoulders. I would love to know what had happened.

During the centuries-long Hungarian rule, there was no compulsory school attendance in the West Carpathians and so, according to statistics, about 60 per cent of the population was still illiterate after World War I. The interest of the Hungarian landlords was exclusively devoted to the forest and the hunt. The life of the locals was extremely primitive. Only after World War I, under Czech rule, was compulsory education introduced.

People's knowledge of world history was so limited that a Rusnak asked my mother in 1935; "Is it true that Hitler married a daughter of the Austrian Emperor Franz Josef?" What a question.

Most of the employees at Čonak came from Bereznik, a small farming village about two kilometres away. A little further away, at the end of the valley, was the larger town of Kerecky. During times of rain and snow the unpaved roads between the two villages would be ankle-deep in mud for months. The families of a few hundred small farmers lived in simple log or brick huts with their animals and survived modestly on their livestock and some farming. Most of them also practised a craft. And in every small village, there is a small, timber-built Russian Orthodox Church to this day. Religion is a big part of life.

Back then the mayor's house in Kerecky also served as a post office and was simply the most splendid house in the town. The stocky rotund mayor, a power-hungry and very nosy man, read every item of incoming mail and then decided what should be passed on to the recipient and what should just be thrown away. He demanded that every guest arriving at Čonak report to him. At the mercy of his favours and to maintain good relations with him, you had to shower him with all sorts of gifts.

Life became a lot busier for the mayor when, in 1872, a railway line was opened from Budapest into the Ukraine, via Munkács, Uzhgorod all the way to Lemberg, now known as L'viv. Munkács, the train stop for Čonak, became the new commercial capital of the Trans-Carpathian region, which meant the family property became more accessible and commercially viable, because Čonak could now be reached from Dresden within two days. For the Schönberg family this meant a horse-drawn-carriage ride from home to Dresden, then a train to Munkács and then another horse-drawn carriage ride for about 30 kilometres to Čonak, which made family visits easier and visiting guests more frequent.

Very soon after her marriage, Emma discovered that life in this unspoiled bit of nature with its people appealed much more to her than the social life back in Germany. Every stay was prolonged to the maximum. But all was not well in this idyllic part of the world: before World War I, Russian partisans crossed the Carpathians frequently and rumours of plundering hordes ousting farmers from their farms, terrified the local community. But Emma was oblivious to it or did not mind. No telegrams from Germany could persuade her to leave Čonak as quickly as possible. She felt at home and she had no intention of simply running away – from whom? She had never been frightened in Čonak: "Such nonsense, just rumours and the imaginings of the superstitious Rusnaks." The Partisan War with its asymmetrical warfare left her cold. She stayed until the very last moment. Only when she heard shots fired by some Partisan fighters echoing through the *Schreigasse* up to the main house did she give the order to hitch two horses to the wagon. She jumped onto the wagon, took the reins and, cracking her whip, galloped out of the courtyard. One Partisan, who had already got close enough to the house to see her riding off, loaded his gun and aimed at her. Just like a Wild West movie. Two bullets narrowly missed killing her, shredding her hat.

That was Emma, nicknamed the 'Carpathian Witch', the mother of my grandmother.

In the following years, 15,000 German residents were expelled – Emma was one of them. For five years, from 1917 to 1922, the Russian Civil War between the 'reds' and the 'whites', who were supported from abroad, raged in the Ukraine. Ultimately Leon Trotsky (the head of the Red Army) declared the independence of the Ukraine and began to bring order to the disunity and chaos amongst the various indigenous groups.

Since Emma's escape from Čonak, there had been no contact with the beloved estate in the Carpathians. Her husband Donald also missed the wilderness and the shooting, particularly during the deer-rutting season. Together with his friend Count Szápáry, he decided to lease a hunting estate in Austria, in Göriach in Lungau/Salzburg, where the world was still well ordered. This connection would play a significant role again years later. With feelings of nostalgia, another long journey from Germany to a remote valley in the Austrian mountains kept the memory of visiting Čonak alive.

Hunting party in Čonak.

The devastating result of World War I was 8.5 million dead soldiers, among them young men of the Schönberg family, and so the medieval castle of Oberreinsberg – not too far from Herzogswalde – fell unexpectedly into Donald's lap. Despite now owning a romantic medieval castle, Emma only dreamt of returning to the Carpathian Mountains as soon as possible.

Many years passed before Emma could risk the journey back to her beloved Čonak. We are now in the year 1922, Emma is 60 years old, her two children grown up and married. There was absolutely nothing that could keep her in Germany any longer.

Hermann the chief gamekeeper with a stag trophy.

Motherly love

*When you work ore long enough,
it eventually becomes steel*

My grandmother, Luisella Emma Christina von Schönberg, was born in Dresden on 18th May, 1888. For the Chinese it would have been a very happy birth date and full of good omens. But my grandmother had one birth defect – she was a girl! Her 26-year-old mother was so disappointed that she had had a daughter, that she immediately put this newly born bundle into the arms of a wet nurse. Not even her mother's milk was granted to her, which wasn't so unusual in those times. And so the life of Luisella, my grandmother, began.

To understand the illogical, self-destructive actions of Emma's daughter, I had to look into her childhood for clues, which opened many doors for modern psychoanalysis: the lack of maternal love cast a shadow over her whole life. Nowadays her problems could probably be solved with psychotherapy – but would she ever have gone into therapy if she had lived in today's world? Sigmund Freud, the father of psychoanalysis, lived in Vienna from 1891 to 1938, at the same time as my grandmother. But it can be assumed that she gave little credence to his revolutionary theories and would have called such nonsense 'hocus-pocus'. She was a strong woman who had her own theories about life and would not have talked about personal feelings nor attributed any importance to them. "You have to adapt to the path of life prescribed by birth, whether you wanted it or not – this is your fate and you had better get on with it." So 'the subconscious' had a free hand over her life, and as an adult she rebelled against all conventions and chose a most complicated and tragic path. What a shame; Sigmund Freud would have had an interesting time with my grandmother on his couch.

The unwanted daughter was left with her mother's parents in Frankfurt, where she was dressed in the finest clothes, learned to eat off bone china with fine silver cutlery and was taught the best manners for her life's journey. She had her own maid – maybe I should say her own slave – who had to guess her every wish. Apart from maternal love, she lacked nothing, but that was the very thing she longed for the most. So Luisella was educated according to the high standards of the family, which meant she did not have to attend a state school but was taught by a private tutor at home and took exams at the end of every school year. Luisella was an attentive student who listened and learned well.

Because she didn't go to school and initially had no siblings, she lacked any contact with other children. Her grandparents were loving but reserved and so there was no one to play with or laugh with or just to be silly with at home. It would have been good for her to have other children around, as she was inherently serious and conscientious. To be with her mother was a rare occurrence. She learned from a very early age to trust her instinct and rely on herself: "Oh *Kindchen*, just rely on yourself," she often said to me.

As soon as she was five or six years old, she was allowed to make the exciting journey to Čonak with her maid during the summer holidays. That's when she finally saw her mother again. But she was greeted by Emma almost like a stranger, without an embrace, very stiffly and formally, and just kissed her mother's hand.

Hunting was a sport for men from the upper classes and also a great passion of the men within my family. The physical challenges of a hunt depended on the hunting grounds in that area. In Čonak, if you pursued the trail of an animal, it could take you through the forest for hours, crisscrossing it and sometimes hiking through snow. To follow a bear track made your heart race at its fastest. Another variation was to sit in a raised hide and wait for the wildlife to come by. Depending on the stock of wildlife and the season, there was always something to hunt and shoot in Čonak. Every evening after the hunt, there were endless debates amongst the hunters, with pipe, cigar or cigarettes. The later the hour, the more exciting the stories became. Čonak was simply a paradise in a man's world. During the rutting season, Emma's husband Donald was one of the many hunting guests to arrive in Čonak. And when he tried to take charge, give orders or bring about some changes, he was banging his head against a brick wall, as Emma was now emancipated and sure of herself. After all, it was Emma who had trained all the staff, who knew all their concerns and wishes and who attended to the fields and cattle. But after a successful hunt, when fresh venison filled the cellars and the dining table with delightful aromas, and the free-flowing wine loosened the atmosphere, their married life returned to bliss. *Vater* (Father) Donald, as he was called in the family, happily wrapped his arms around Emma. And so, the deer-rutting season of 1894 had its consequences. As usual, when the men boarded the train back to Dresden in late autumn, Emma remained in Čonak. Again, she could not be persuaded to come back home for Christmas. Snow covered the house and yard; temperatures frequently went down to -30° Celsius and heating the house would be challenging, in spite of the limitless supply of firewood. Emma stayed. The *Schreigasse*, which allowed her to shout her orders down to the administration building, was especially welcome during that particular winter, because she wanted to avoid slipping on the steep icy path. After all, she was harbouring a life-changing secret.

Christmas with her staff in Čonak was more to Emma's liking than being with her family. She mused, "*Ach*, my daughter is in good hands with my parents and they don't need me." Not another thought crossed her mind about the family back home.

In February, when her husband came back again for the winter hunt, he saw immediately what her secret was: Emma was five months pregnant.

Overjoyed, he wanted to take her back to Germany right away, so nothing could go wrong with the birth, but Emma refused.

In the following weeks and months, he sent one telegram after another to persuade her to give birth in Germany.

The curious mayor-cum-postmaster-cum-spy read all the telegrams with great interest. Maybe he threw some of the telegrams away because they were always about the same subject: "Please come home immediately."

The mayor had a weakness for Emma because she would let him fish in the river and every now and then she would give him a nice piece of venison.

Meanwhile the senior doctor at Munkács Hospital, who was the first to get the news, was trembling in fear and anticipation: would Emma come to the maternity ward in his hospital?

Up to now, he had been able to escape quickly when Emma came for her scheduled inspections. He was still suffering from the shock and the lasting repercussions of the young Emma's behaviour during the hospital's opening ceremony. At the inauguration of the new hospital to which Emma had contributed large sums of money, she proceeded to do the unthinkable: she was so appalled when she saw the dirt around the entrance and on the stairs that she slapped the senior doctor in the face in front of everyone. This was truly a humiliation beyond belief!

Now it was plain for everybody to see who wore the trousers in the Schönberg family. After this catastrophic beginning for the senior doctor of the new hospital, he had the good fortune to find a stern nurse who got on well with Emma and who flattered her in such a way as to keep money flowing into the hospital coffers.

To everybody's surprise, Emma had no intention of giving birth to the child at the hospital. She had decided to bring her child into the world at home, just as all the local women did. On one hand she might have already adapted to the primitive life, identified herself with her peers and didn't think twice about it, or worry about any negative consequences. On the other hand, she might have wanted to prove to her family back in Germany how strong and independent she had become. It was in her nature to be stubborn and refuse any advice.

Nobody could reason with the now 33-year old mother of Luisella. No pleading from her husband was persuasive enough to make her leave Čonak. And so, on 27th June, 1895, the *Panika*, the 'Lady of Čonak', gave birth to a long-awaited son with only a midwife by her side. No family, no doctor – just like any other local woman. The slightest complication could have meant death. She did not want to acknowledge this – she did it her way. What emotions brought her to this decision – to bring a child into the world with nothing but a midwife and a petroleum lamp, in the wilderness, without running water or a doctor? I would like to have looked into her soul.

Overjoyed at the birth of a healthy son, it was only fitting for Donald to purchase a new hunting rifle, the first Winchester with smokeless cartridges.

Just as Emma's personal development had followed an unstoppable path, the political situation around her had changed too: the year 1903 was the year of the birth of the Bolsheviks. Bolshevik literally means 'majority', which crystallised into followers of Lenin and opponents of the Czar. They joined together as the Social Democratic Labour Party of Russia. Subsequently, after 1918, they changed their name to the Communist Party of Russia.

But as untouched by events and as blissfully unaware as any seven-year-old girl would be, my grandmother set off to spend the summer in Čonak again. She had been looking forward to it all year. The train journey with her chambermaid, first class, all the way from Frankfurt via Budapest to Munkács, was hugely exciting, changing trains and crossing two borders with strict passport controls. With every passing kilometre she became more and more excited, until at last she saw the coachman waiting with the horse-drawn carriage at Munkács railway station. The next 30 kilometres were the slowest, with endless potholes making the trip dangerous, but also the most exhilarating. It took many hours, which only increased the eager anticipation of arriving at Čonak.

Accustomed to her unloving mother and familiar with her image of a loveless world, Luisella was completely unprepared for what was about to happen. When the carriage was brought up in the wide courtyard in front of the main house, a radiant mother stepped out of the door. She held out her arms – not to welcome her daughter, however, but to show her a surprise: the baby in her arms – her brother.

Completely overwhelmed, the child Luisella suddenly realised how different her mother could be. She fondled, cuddled and kissed the baby in her arms, not taking her eyes off it. Luisella wanted to be treated just like her baby brother; she was longing for her mother's love. Like a puppy dog, she followed her mother all day long, tugging at her skirt to get her attention: she too wanted to be caressed. But her mother only had eyes for her son, 'the heir to the throne'. It was as if her daughter did not exist. Naturally, it did not take long before Luisella became jealous of this little intruder. No matter how hard she tried, she found no empathy in her mother, and, desperately looking for love, she turned to her father, Donald. He was a good-natured man, but he was completely unaccustomed to dealing with little girls. The more she followed him around, the more he withdrew. After cuddling her and allowing her to sit on his lap a few times, his affection was exhausted. "Can't you play with your dolls?" he would say. The surrounding wilderness with its abundance of animals was much more familiar to him, and he was already dreaming of his next hunt.

Nevertheless, they were still humane, and as a consolation Luisella was given a pony. It was hers alone. Now she had something to pamper, kiss and embrace. She fed, brushed and marvelled at her new 'baby'. From that moment on, most of her time was spent in the stable. But when the summer came to an end, she had to leave her beloved pony behind and return to Frankfurt with her maid. Her new-born brother was allowed to stay with his mother in Čonak. Was there no justice in life? She would have given anything to be allowed to stay.

"*Kindchen*, you can always rely on animals: they never let you down, but people do," was one of her oft-repeated pieces of advice. I suspect that her great love of animals came from this early childhood experience. My grandmother would never have abandoned a dog, a cat or any other pet. When her beloved 14-year-old Chimmy, the dog, became so weak that he could no longer walk properly, she took a pistol and shot him herself. In her eyes, this was true love.

In our family, humans were always likened to animals and were given animal nicknames according to their character or appearance. This custom passed down to my father, who gave my brother and me the nickname 'pugs'. Whenever we couldn't be found, it was always "Where are the pugs?" We never asked that question, why we were called 'the pugs'. I view pugs as rather funny-looking, well bred, slightly degenerate dogs. Not scary. The Schönborns, our neighbours in Čonak had two pugs. That could have been one reason. I guess it was a compliment to us, referring to us in terms of pugs.

Many of our friends and family were compared to animals whose character they matched in my parents' imaginations and were referred to accordingly. My most loved aunt was the 'chicken', another aunt was the 'sheep'. The 'trout' was a man with thin wet lips and yellow stumps for teeth that had been damaged by relentless smoking; the 'rutting stag' was a lascivious widower who chased after women and wild animals with the same vigour. A neighbour was the 'snake', a vain uncle was the 'lion'. These nicknames were more familiar to us than their real names, which meant we had to be careful to avoid a slip of the tongue.

Had Luisella been a pretty girl, she might have had a better chance of enchanting her parents. No one had ever said, "Oh, what a sweet little girl." I've tried to imagine how she looked as a child, whether her penetrating blue-grey eyes, attractive and frightening at the same time, were made to pierce through people from birth. However, when I was 12, my grandmother's eyes scared me. According to my mother, she had a sensual mouth and beautiful teeth. In official family photos, as a young woman, she always looked very serious, peering somewhat longingly into the distance. It was neither modern nor elegant at the time to laugh into the camera. If I wanted to be polite, I'd describe her most prominent feature, her nose, as 'striking, classical'. If I wanted to be truly honest, then I would simply say, "She had a big hooked nose," which is well disguised in any photograph. As she became older, she had almost no neck, with no room at all for a three-string pearl necklace.

Her face was the opposite of a doll's face. Describing herself, she would say, "I am an Irish beauty." Why? Had she met an Irish girl who looked like her or admired an Irish beauty? I thought of Frida Kahlo, the Mexican painter, with her bushy black eyebrows that met above her nose, or Luisella's ancestress, Anna Constantia von Cosel, the famous mistress of Augustus the Strong.

Luisella as Panika, Baroness and Baronesa.

With her strong masculine features, my grandmother looked very much like her brother. He was younger by seven years and looked distinguished with his striking facial characteristics. Dressed with a hat, shirt and tie, Luisella could easily have been the older brother. Their short 'Dachshund' legs were not suitable for the catwalk, but, as it turned out later, it was the family's best gift for survival in Russia. She and her brother were short and stocky, which was worse for her brother than for her. But he made up for his lack of height with energy, intellect and the self-assured demeanour of a landlord. The broad, clumsy hands of both siblings were passed down to my father.

Young Luisella's hard masculine appearance made it difficult for Emma, her mother, to find her a suitable husband. All social events were attended; no dance soirée was ignored. She was dressed in the best clothes and adorned with her mother's jewellery. I can't help but make a comparison with animals, when the cows are brought down from the high pastures in the autumn, decorated with flowers and bells, upon their return to the villages. To find a husband was the most important task in a woman's life, because a hundred years ago her career path had only three options: become a wife, a nurse or a nun.

Today my grandmother would have become a successful entrepreneur.

Just get married quickly

When the oil is finished, the lamp goes out

After finishing her formal education, my grandmother was sent to England for a year. That's where she flourished. She said it was the most wonderful time of her life and felt an overwhelming sense of freedom. At last, she was with young people of her own age; she practised sports and became a valuable member of the hockey team. She never wanted to leave England, but her mother summoned her back to Germany saying that she had to 'find a husband and get married'. After a short stay at home, she was sent off to friends in France as a paying guest to polish up her French language skills, which would complete her education. Fluent in three languages, well-mannered and well read, she had become a young lady, marriageable. At the age of 22 it was high time to find her a man. But, although impeccably educated and equipped with the best manners, her appearance and lack of charm made it difficult to attract admirers. I wonder if her piercing eyes and questioning mind scared off the young and innocent.

However, fate struck when the Countess Wurmbrand invited Luisella to a hunting soirée in the state of Lower Austria, which was a long way from Frankfurt. She met a charming officer of the Imperial Austro-Hungarian Army. In his regal hussar's uniform of red jacket, golden epaulettes and tight black trousers, he represented glorious military power at its best. The 'magic of the uniform' not only looked elegant but added sex appeal and mystery; it will always make a man look his best. For Luisella, it was love at first sight.

The officer liked this serious, inquisitive little German girl. Never mind her looks, which were of no importance to him. At the age of 38 he had been around young beauties with bright red lips, strong perfume and lots of small talk for long enough to be able to look beyond all this. He was exhausted and bored with the officer's world and Luisella was like a breath of fresh air blown into his bachelor life. Besides, he was at last thinking of settling down. He enjoyed their conversation about horses and hunting and when he discovered that she was a smoker, he would gallantly light her cigarette. For him, Luisella must have seemed like a gift from heaven: young, rich, an excellent rider (a huge bonus) from a suitably aristocratic family, and a Protestant – because religion still played a big part in the choice of a spouse. Did he fall in love with her? Why not. Maybe it was her sexual aura, which I cannot really explain but I could sense even as a child. With the confidence of an officer, he was soon addressing her using the informal *du* instead of the formal *sie*. (How I wish the German language had the same simple universal 'you' that English has.) He gave her the lovely Viennese-sounding name *Luiserl*.

Emma was thrilled that her daughter had found a suitable gentleman and Luisella and her officer were quickly married in Dresden on 21st February, 1911. My grandmother was 23 years old; her husband was 15 years older. Thus, the soldier Moriz Baron von Ditfurth became my grandfather. Although born into a German family, my grandfather spoke German with a Hungarian accent, since he had grown up in Hungary and had gone to school there. Because of his love of Hungary, he preferred to write his first name, Moriz, the Hungarian way – without a 't', which would have been the German spelling.

His father, nicknamed 'Iron Max', was married to a Croatian aristocrat called Kušević de Blacko and lived comfortably in the Balkans. Iron Max rejected his German relatives and Germany altogether. The Ditfurth family was a true product of the Imperial Austro-Hungarian Empire. Luisella now had a mother-in-law who lived neither in Vienna nor in Germany and didn't stand in her way at all. For the second time in her life, she felt an exuberant sense of freedom. The world was her oyster.

According to family tradition, the Ditfurths had been proud, professional soldiers for many generations – that is, officers with commanding authority over junior officers and the ranks. As a result of the Coalition Wars, professional soldiers had to attend a military academy in Bavaria and additional compulsory field training. As fully established mercenary soldiers, they were ready to fight in any army. In 1809, during the 5th Coalition War, the Ditfurth family came into contact with Austria for the first time. As the protector of Bavaria, Napoleon became an enemy of Austria. On 10th April, 1809, Austria indirectly attacked France, which was an ally of Bavaria. It was during that war that the name Ditfurth became prominent: Colonel Karl von Ditfurth fought for Napoleon and the King of Bavaria, who ruled over Tyrol, then a separate state within Austria. During his nine-year rule, the King of Bavaria did not keep his promise to protect the people. The people of Tyrol, a hardy mountain folk, found in Andreas Hofer a superb leader for their rebellion against exploitation. France, as the ally of Bavaria, was dragged into war. The First Battle of Bergisel began on 12th April, 1809, and lasted two days. Under the command of the Austrian Archduke Karl, when Austrians were basically

Luisella and Moriz early in their married life.

fighting against Austrians, the Archduke had to accept heavy losses. On the very first day of this battle, the 35-year-old Karl von Ditfurth was wounded, but bravely continued commanding the battle from his stretcher, until he fainted and died the same evening in a hospital in Innsbruck. An oil painting of this epic battle showing Karl lying on the stretcher still in commanding posture is on display at the History Museum in Innsbruck. He fought as a German for Napoleon, in the name of Bavaria, against Austria. How confusing is that? A year later Napoleon married the Austrian Emperor's daughter Marie-Louise: European politics of the time!

A hundred years later Luisella, as the young bride of a Ditfurth, arrived with great expectations in the cosmopolitan *Kaiserstadt* (Emperor's city), Vienna, the most vibrant and cultured metropolis in Europe, leaving London and Paris out in the cold. Since 1867, thanks to an Imperial Decree, Jews had been given the same citizenship rights as Austrians. This brought about an unforeseen wave of immigration of Eastern Jews, who would no longer suffer discrimination and consequently flocked in their thousands, to Vienna.

Within two generations they had assimilated perfectly and had become rich and respectable: they led luxurious lifestyles, had servants, frequented the best restaurants in town, became patrons of the arts and supporters of all cultural activities. When my grandmother arrived in Vienna, these immigrants were well established, had many titles to their names and lived in splendid marble palaces along the *Ringstrasse*, the most prestigious street in Vienna.

By 1910, Vienna had the second largest Jewish population in the world after New York. At that time, Jews dominated every facet of public life: 71 per cent of the financial world was Jewish, 65 per cent of lawyers, 59 per cent of doctors and half of all journalists. The *Neue Freie Presse* was written by Jewish journalists and published by Jewish owners.

My grandmother had fond memories of the Jews she had known as a child in Čonak. Now in Vienna, the Jewish street vendors who pushed their loaded carts into Vienna's courtyards shouting *handlee* ('here to bargain') especially enthralled her. They had everything from furs, carpets, watches and gold chains to sheets, scissors and pots, and if they did not have something, they would bring it tomorrow. Luisella almost felt as if she was back in Čonak. What a welcome change to the stiff, formal life in Germany.

Luisella was now the wife of a Lieutenant Colonel of the Imperial Austro-Hungarian army who spoke Viennese with a Hungarian accent. It sounded so soft and charming. The young couple moved into a large apartment at the *Reitlehrer Institut* (Calvary Institute) in the centre of Vienna. As *Rittmeister* in the Theresianum Military Academy in Wiener Neustadt, a suburb of Vienna, Moriz was to take over the management of the world-famous Spanish Riding School at the end of his active military career. A big black-and-white photograph in a heavy brown wooden frame, showing Moriz sitting on a *Lipizzaner* (white horse), hung in our bathroom. Whenever I brushed my teeth, Moriz was watching me. It was self-evident that they had their own horses, which were housed in elegant stables in the Prater, a huge park full of chestnut trees, lawns and riding tracks, amusement parks and grand avenues. The horses could be ridden on any occasion. Luisella sat just as tightly in the saddle as her husband, but on Sundays they rode comfortably in the horse-drawn carriage in the main avenue of the Prater – it was the grand outing, the time to be seen.

The rank of Lieutenant Colonel granted my grandfather a batman (a personal servant), which made his life very pleasant and uncomplicated. And just as Luisella had had her maid as a child, she now found herself a 16-year-old peasant girl, Pepi, from the state of Styria. At that time, Pepi could not have foreseen that she would accompany her new mistress through all the ups and downs of life in a sort of obedient dependency.

The newly married couple often went to the opera, my grandmother proudly wearing the diamond earrings of Anna Constantia von Cosel, the famous mistress of Augustus the Strong. (I will get to their lives a little later.) During winter outings, she protected herself from the cold with a simple Loden coat that was lined with the most exquisite fur, a popular understatement of elegance amongst the aristocracy. Together they enjoyed all the pleasures this most cultured and sophisticated city had to offer.

But all too soon my grandmother came to realise that her life was not evolving as she had imagined. Moriz was used to the independent military life and had no intention of suddenly changing his lifestyle to accommodate the needs of his young wife. She should just live happily by his side. He continued to go out alone, or rather with his older brother, Niki. With his brother, who was his best friend, he instinctively spoke Hungarian, because they both felt most comfortable in the Hungarian language. To pay attention to his young wife and to speak German in her presence did not enter his mind. She was just like another piece of furniture in the room. My grandmother was therefore excluded from any chatter between the brothers. Never a quitter, already fluent in English, French and Dutch, she threw herself into the new task of learning Hungarian.

But, as if she was jinxed, the Hungarian language remained foreign and incomprehensible to her. Her hopes and expectations of finally finding love and understanding in her new life in Vienna faded into the distance. The happy life together with her new husband that she had imagined was very short lived. In letters to her friends she wrote, "I have good manners,

Luisella and Franzl.

I know how to behave, I know how to dress, but Moriz always leaves me alone at home." Instead of going out in a threesome (with his brother), she usually sat alone in the beautiful apartment and waited. When her charming husband finally came home, which could sometimes be early in the morning, he always kissed her hand gallantly, never thinking to give any explanation or excuse. Today, no woman would put up with that. So Luisella, quite unexpectedly, was alone again, without company, just as she had been as a child many years before in Frankfurt. Her longing for love remained unfulfilled. But her great fortune was that a child was born exactly nine months after their marriage: a son, my father, Franz Dietrich XV, on 8th December, 1911, in Vienna. She could now cuddle her baby, as she had done with her pony when she was a child, hold it close and tight. Her life had finally found meaning – she called him Franzl. At that time, she did not know that he was to remain her only child: the dream of having many children came to an end after a miscarriage. Fate had dealt her another hard blow.

World War I 1914-1918

*When three men are of one mind,
yellow earth becomes gold*

❋

Three years into their marriage, World War I broke out and Moriz, the career military man, was conscripted at the age of 41. With the help of a lot of propaganda, enthusiasm for the War was fostered, patriotism was stirred up, and normal everyday life had an air of excitement. As a Lieutenant Colonel of the Imperial Austro-Hungarian army, he was summoned to the *Isonzo* front in Italy and assigned to the Field Marshal, the highest ranked officer, Baron Svetozar Boroević of Bojna as adjutant. Both men were full of expectations, only to experience later one of the most horrific human tragedies of World War I. It did not deliver the expected heroism and glory, but rather turned these patriotic men into cannon fodder of the enemy. During the 12 battles that raged against the Italians on the 60-kilometre-long *Isonzo* riverfront, Field Marshal Boroević and Moriz fretted more over strategically important moves on maps than over dead soldiers in the firing line. However, the negative reports and alarming messages from the front line gave them sleepless nights.

Boroević was nicknamed the 'Lion of Isonzo' because of his boldness, and perhaps also because of his great vanity. The two men supported each other and shared the heavy burden of the War. My grandfather told the following story: When the Archduke of Austria, who was the Commander in Chief, came to the *Isonzo* front to carry out an inspection, he briefly looked at the maps and listened to Boroević, who began to explain every step his troops had taken in pedantic, minute detail, which bored the Archduke in no time at all. He said, "Boroević knows all this a lot better than I do, so let's go to the room next door, Ditfurth, and you can cheer me up with some jokes."

Jokes and the military went hand in hand, probably a necessary distraction from reality in times of war. My grandfather collected jokes, as had his father, and my father continued the tradition. The jokes were written down in small leather-bound books so they could easily be carried around at all times. It was the Ditfurth family's most precious heirloom.

The Second World War too created a boom in political jokes – every day there were at least 10 new ones. My father was enthusiastic and wrote them all down with code names, such as *Hi, Eich, Him, Gö*, so it was easy to work out who was who (Hitler, Eichmann, Himmler, Göring). If they had been discovered during a house search, my father would have had nothing to laugh about, even the threat of the death penalty could not deter him from noting a good joke. During our escape from the Russians at Easter 1945, the saving of the joke collection was, needless to say, a top priority.

In order to extend this 'valuable collection' my father paid five *schillings* to everyone who told him a worthwhile joke. Every now and then my brother brought home a good joke from school, but mostly the chauffeurs had the best jokes. When we lived in Tenneck and Prince Friedrich Leopold of Prussia (a nephew of the last German Emperor) lived in the neighbouring valley, the *Imlau Tal*, my father would be 'summoned' for joke recitals. There was always an exquisite supper with rare wines before the servants were sent away and the evening was finished off with lots of laughter over the saucy jokes.

The collection of my father's joke books.

But back to World War I. Some time after the end of the War, Boroević gave Moriz a portrait of himself done in chalk as a reminder of the years they had spent together during the War. This picture hung in our dining room in Vienna. Imposing and very stern, he looked down on our dining table for many years. For him, the end of the War was even more of a personal tragedy than for Moriz. He was the only Serbo-Croat by birth who, in the history of the Imperial Monarchy, had ever been elevated to the rank of Field Marshal, the highest military rank. After the War, he offered himself as a free adviser to the new South Slavic State. His Slavic heart and pride were mortally wounded when not only was his offer rejected, but entry into the newly-created state of Yugoslavia was denied him. He was no longer needed, no longer wanted, no longer respected. He could not have fallen from a higher pedestal and he died impoverished and embittered in Austria two years after the War ended.

I had long forgotten the details of Austrian history, so when I did some deeper research into the battles on the *Isonzo* front, I was taken aback to find that 65 million soldiers were under arms during the War, of whom eight-and-a-half million died, with a further seven million civilians dead, and 21 million wounded. If today's wars are about technology, back then it was about bravery, human sacrifice and a great loss of blood.

Since Luisella's husband was away at war, my 26-year-old grandmother had to take her fate into her own hands. She could choose to make life easy for herself by simply locking up the Viennese apartment and returning home to Saxony with the status of wife and mother. She could live comfortably in one of the two family estates in the security of her German family. But she had grown very fond of Vienna, even though the cosmopolitan, clean, cultured city was slowly sinking into chaos. She cherished her independence above all. Grandmother Luisella chose the more uncomfortable path – even if by our standards today it sounds most luxurious – of staying in Vienna with her three-year-old son Franzl, Pepi and a cook. In Vienna she wanted to gain a foothold, to assert herself and contribute wherever she could. This was her home now and the idea of giving up her independence filled her with horror.

Like so many women of that time, she attended a Red Cross course and passionately embraced the new challenge of becoming a nurse. After all, she was intelligent, diligent and tidy; she passed all the exams with distinction and was immediately put to good use. With great gusto and energy, she took on the new task of standing on her own two feet in times of need and despair.

During the four years of World War I, my grandparents met only a few times a year at the castle of their friend in Carinthia. With every reunion they grew further apart. Both lived in their separate worlds full of worries and anxieties. Little Franzl had become a big part of his mother's life, at her side everywhere she went. Under the protection of this strong woman, who had adapted easily to the new circumstances of hunger and distress, he felt little of the chaos of war. He had a happy childhood, and the absence of his father did not worry him. Besides, in those days, fathers had little to do with their young children as this was seen as a woman's job. There was never a harsh word between the parents, because it was simply not done to speak rudely or argue in the presence of children and servants.

The outcome of the War was unpredictable. With every day, with every news bulletin from the front, life became more difficult for my grandfather, while for his Luisella it led to more confidence and independence. Rarely did she think of her husband or wonder how he was coping. Sporadic letters came from the front, always with bad news. While her husband was becoming more and more depressed, she was growing in strength, mastering her new life superbly without a husband. It came as no surprise when it was rumoured within the family that a young doctor, who was working with her in the same hospital, had become her lover.

When in 1917 a catastrophic famine struck Vienna and basic food items such as bread, milk and butter were no longer available, my grandmother in conjunction with the Red Cross, organised a collective transport by train to the Netherlands for 200 children. Relatives and friends accommodated the Viennese children wherever there was still something to eat. My father, Franzl, was always at her side and happy with all the other children. He liked to play hide and seek on the train. For him, the War was more adventure than catastrophe. Through her tireless work at the Red Cross, Luisella showed what she was made of; she earned great respect, praise and recognition. She felt on top of the world, having a fulfilling mission, a healthy child and a lover.

In 1918, after four years of bloody battles, the War finally came to an end and the First Republic was announced on 11th November. The question now was whether the dwarf state of Austria could be viable with six million people. The Habsburg monarchy, with a population of 52 million people and after Russia, the second largest country in Europe, had collapsed. The devastated population with wounded, unemployed, desperate people, who had survived the War, was left to rebuild their country. Amongst them were Moriz and a young German corporal, who was born in Austria, called Adolf Hitler.

My grandparent's marriage did not thrive after the War. Eventually Luisella's lover had to vacate his place because, after all, she was married. With the end of the monarchy, the status of the military plummeted and was much diminished. Eight years earlier the man she had married had been a proud hussar in a red jacket with golden epaulettes; now, Moriz, a defeated soldier and a broken man, returned to Vienna. The previous world order was destroyed. No more uniform, no more batman, no officer's apartment, no work and no recognition. The little money he had possessed had been put into war bonds, as was expected of every patriotic Austrian at the time. Now they had become worthless. All these factors combined had made my grandmother lose more and more respect for her husband. On top of that, my grandmother, who was naturally penny-pinching, had her own ideas about a matrimonial household: she demanded that each of them look after themselves in spite of her still having a small fortune. Moriz only had a modest military pension. "Oh, he'll just have to find a way to survive. After all, I am providing for Franzl." Was it her secret revenge for the many lonely evenings and the Hungarian language?

By chance and through old connections, Moriz finally found a suitable apartment that he could afford – because it was his responsibility and duty to provide the family home – in the Lower Belvedere, Rennweg 6. It was spacious, with seven rooms, a lavatory, a kitchen, but no bathroom. This did not bother them, because they were accustomed to bathing in a large plastic tub – just as they had done in Čonak. So, after dinner on Wednesdays and Sundays, the designated 'bath days', the tub was placed in the large kitchen. My father held on to this ritualistic schedule all his life, even after we had a bath with running water.

Always a practical thinker, Luisella bought a goat, which she tied to a pear tree in the garden with a long cord, so she had daily fresh milk for her son. She purchased chickens and planted a vegetable garden, which made them almost self-sufficient. My father raved about the apartment all his life: he could walk to school at the Theresianum – a prestigious high school for boys – and to the ice-skating club. He could ride his bike in the park and when snow fell outside, he cycled in the long corridor in the apartment. He was happy.

The many hunting trophies adorning the wall-papered walls were a constant reminder of Čonak and when their melancholic thoughts went back to Čonak, they wondered how all the employees with their families and of course all the animals, had survived the political turmoil.

It was reported that in 1919, Ukrainian Cossacks under the leadership of Simon Petilura wanted to conquer Munkács, but were forced back by a Jewish civilian guerrilla army of war veterans. As a temporary solution, the Czech and Romanian army shared the city of Munkács, which meant that you needed a passport if you wanted to cross certain streets. The peaceful coexistence of the various ethnic groups in this ancient Austro-Hungarian Habsburg empire had been destroyed forever.

As for so many others, the situation for Moriz was sad. The promised reward for his long and successful military career was the position of Principal of the Spanish Riding School. This dream job was now gone and he had to find a way of making a living just like the rest of the 400,000 unemployed Austrians. At the age of 46 he enrolled in an accounting course and hoped for a new career. He applied for a job as an accountant targeting what remained of the military. But despite all his connections, Moriz did not find a job. It was a desperate time. He had one more problem: as a 'Hungarian at heart', and because the state pension for Hungarians was somewhat higher, Moriz had opted for Hungarian nationality rather than Austrian, a choice every citizen could make after the collapse of the monarchy. But it meant that he was now a foreigner in socialist Vienna.

With every day that passed, the economic crisis became a bigger problem; with unemployment rising to 18 per cent, the government's debt could not be met. It was practically impossible to get a work permit. Moriz felt old and superfluous, a feeling readily confirmed by his Luisella. The prospect of improvement within Austria and within the Ditfurth family faded with each passing day. Since Luisella only cared for the education of their son, she did not pay a *schilling* towards the household. With great pleasure she played the trump card, 'money'.

Moriz's beloved older brother could not cope with the collapse of the existing world order and took his own life at the end of the War. Moriz lost his best friend and confidant.

My father

You shall not eat bread if you haven't earned it

❋

My father was an only child. Spoiled – yes, of course, it couldn't have been any other way as an only child. With motherly love, Luisella ruled him firmly. He was in all aspects a dream son, for not only was he a handsome boy, he also came home year after year with distinctions in his school reports. Little boys' pranks were tolerated and thought funny, because Franzl was otherwise always obedient.

When he became a high school student at the Theresianum in Vienna, which at the time was regarded as a strict and elitist school, he still came home every year with a certificate of distinction. He had a very good memory and would have considered it a waste of time not to pay attention in class. Writing letters was a big part of life back then, and his mother wrote that these untroubled times were the most rewarding of her life. Franzl was so attentive at school because he did not want to waste any more time studying after school, when he was busy having fun. Playing ice hockey was the first priority in winter. It was he who introduced ice hockey as a school sport to the Theresianum. As a striker for the *Wiener Eislaufverein*, he later took part in international matches.

My grandmother wrote in her last letter from Russia:

> "I sometimes froze my soul in the Viennese wind, but went again and again, because it was so entertaining to watch them play."

Not only that, but she knew that for boys a great deal of sport is important to keep their testosterone under control, and she also knew that he would make many friends through his sporting activities. Naturally sporty, my father was a good tennis player and was popular with everybody, a trait that saw him invited to stay at the castles of various friends and relatives. But his real passion in life became hunting.

As a city boy, he spent his holidays either in Čonak or in the Lungau, always in the mountains, never by the sea. But swimming was simply part of his sports education, which is why my grandmother went to the Dianabad, then the most famous public swimming pool in Vienna. He was about ten years old and had the misfortune to have a swimming instructor who believed that being thrown in at the deep end was the best teaching method, with the maxim 'swim or die'! This moment of indescribable panic remained in my father's memory for the rest of his life and he never ventured into the water deeper than chest height; he would do a few strokes and then go back to the shore greatly relieved. The irony of fate was that he married a record-holding swimmer, my mother, who had sworn as a young girl, "I will never marry a non-swimmer."

When Vienna once again was plagued by a terrible invasion of head lice my father came home from school with lice crawling all over his head. My grandmother, always practical, shaved his head bare, so that no more lice could feel at home. My father then acquired the nickname *Eierdidi* (Egghead) at school and suffered terribly as the only bald-headed boy in his class. But, as far as his mother was concerned, it was quite out of the question to pay attention to such 'nonsense'.

Family life in the garden of Luisella and Moriz's home in Vienna.

Franzl with orphaned wolves.

My well-to-do grandmother, of course, was very eager to turn Franzl into the perfect gentleman. This project failed miserably, no matter how often she preached, "You have to wait for the lady of the house to start eating before you eat; you have to ask if you may smoke; you must let ladies go through a door first," – to name only a few basic social rules. It was to no avail; at no time in his life did he adhere to any of these. Was it in rebellion against his mother, or because it simply didn't matter to him?

Uncle Wolf, my grandmother's younger brother, constantly complained about his nephew's bad manners, which very much annoyed her, for after all, he was her 'Wunderkind'. But it made no difference, my father behaved as he pleased. My mother also failed in her attempts to teach him manners. It could have been total self-absorption, or did such strict rules not fit his character?

Dancing was another part of the drill for someone growing up in Vienna, and so his mother took him as a 13-year-old *Eierdidi* to a private dance school at the palatial home of one of their friends. The result was much the same as with swimming – he hated dancing and never became a good dancer. He was too young, and, with a shaved head and no natural rhythm, he became the laughing stock of the girls.

Franzl was 15 when the first traffic light was installed in Vienna in 1926, by the Opera House. Cars were then the most exciting technical development. My father knew every car in Vienna. He wanted to become a racing driver and eagerly awaited his 18th birthday to take the driving test. "Such nonsense, you can just get it right out of your head", was the verdict from my grandmother. The dream of becoming a racing driver was killed in its infancy.

My father was quite humble, and so, after getting his High School Certificate with distinction, he wished only for a motorcycle. My grandmother could easily have fulfilled his heart's desire as money was not the issue. Was it meanness or power? Or fear of accidents? For whatever reason she did not grant his wish, which would have strengthened his love for her. Instead, this unfulfilled desire became a lasting thorn. As a student and being a Hungarian citizen, he was unable to earn any pocket money but was dependent on his mother's handouts. By now unemployment in Vienna had risen to about 20 per cent. His mother insisted that he study agriculture, although forestry would have been more appropriate for taking over the legacy of Čonak. In fact, history would have been his desired subject. And throughout his life, he fantasised about cars and racing them. It was not until he was 50 years old that my father had enough money to fulfil his dream: he bought a black Porsche. He was an excellent driver, but he observed the rules of traffic rather like the rules of good manners. If a traffic light was red but he could see there was nothing in the way, he simply took off. He also adhered to the speed limits according to his own scale. If he was stopped by the police here and there, he excused himself with an innocent twinkle of the eye and pointed to the Automobile Club medal, which testified to decades of accident-free driving; this would usually result in a simple warning.

Winter hunt in Čonak with Hermann (Franzl is on the right in the picture).

Franzl with a stag trophy.

For the time being, hunting remained Franzl's greatest passion. During the holidays in Čonak, the hunters showed him how to handle guns so that he could go on hunts without a parent, accompanied only by a hunter. At thirteen, he was declared old enough to shoot his first roebuck; his passion for hunting grew into an obsession and by the time he reached his early twenties, he had been gripped by so-called hunting fever. At the sight of a deer, a fox, a bird, any game at all, he started to tremble uncontrollably and was no longer able to aim the gun at his target and shoot.

Among the numerous trophies he collected, he was proudest of a bear he shot. For days he and a trusted stalker followed the tracks of the bear through the thawing snowfields, until he got his chance and killed him with a single shot. The bear skin hung above my bed in Vienna. Hunting constantly swirled around his head. Luckily, he possessed some writing skills, which gave him some pocket money with the opportunity to account his adventures in the Carpathian Mountains for a German hunting magazine.

During World War II, these hunting trophies with so many memories attached, were saved by my father with utmost care and whoever came to our apartment in Vienna was greeted by a pair of huge deer antlers hanging in the stairwell. There was no room left inside the apartment. In the narrow entrance way every guest came across a mounted wild boar's head. The rest of the hunting trophies decorated the walls right up to the ceiling. The trophy of Donald's world-record chamois, shot in 1901, was prominently displayed there as well. Now it adorns a wall in my hunting enthusiast nephew's flat.

With the loss of Čonak, my father also lost his passion for hunting and no longer found any joy in it. To be just a 'guest hunter' without being able to reciprocate was not something he could enjoy. Moreover, no other hunting ground could replace the romance and the wilderness of the Carpathians. So, he shot his last chamois on the steep slopes of the Tennengebirge, which became our new home at the end of World War II. At the age of 37, he would say good-bye to hunting forever. With the maxim 'Times have changed', skiing became his new passion.

My father, the skier.

The reign of terror

A butterfly knows no snow

At his wedding in 1885, Donald could not have foreseen that his new wife, Emma, who had no hunting ambitions, would succumb to the charm of the wilderness and would be captivated by the primitive lifestyle.

The turmoil of World War I ended with the Winter Battle and the defeat of the Bolsheviks in the Carpathian region on 15th April, 1922. The time had come for Emma to return to Čonak. The destruction the Bolsheviks left behind had completely demoralised the local population and Emma was welcomed as a heroine. It was well remembered how she had left Čonak at the last moment four years previously, brandishing her whip, bullets flying. What had once been a perfect sanctuary had become a devastated land after the years of chaos that had reigned over land and people. Emma was horrified when she saw the demolition of the houses, grounds, gardens and fields left by the endless crossfire between Bolsheviks and the Red Army. She became even angrier when the new Czech administration made her responsible for the repairs of the damage to the property.

A political decision was made to change the government (from Hungarian to Czechoslovakian) after World War I, without taking into consideration either history or people. The secret goal was clearly the total exploitation of the land with its rich agriculture.

Intimidated by Emma's reputation, the newly appointed Czech tax officer took weeks to build up the courage for a visit. Because of many years of complicated circumstances with an absentee landlord, he now wanted to recover Čonak's outstanding taxes. When he was finally granted a visit, he did not anticipate a good outcome. As soon as he entered the house, he was greeted by Emma screaming: "I have no intention of paying a single penny of taxes since the property has been completely devastated, and it will cost a fortune to get everything back in order." The Czechs had only taken over the administration after the destruction, but Emma did not care. "Do not ever come back to me!"

Emma slammed the door in his face. Trembling all over, he crept away and never came back. And Emma did not pay any taxes. Every tax demand was torn up contemptuously and thrown in the wastepaper basket next to her desk. Subsequent tax officers suffered the same fate. Čonak was at war with the new government and this became an untenable situation. Emma's husband, Donald, who had to look after the German estates, did not have the strength to resolve this embarrassing situation. Whenever he cautiously took up the matter with Emma, he received a barrage of invective about politics. When Donald died in 1926 with no prospect of a resolution, four years had already elapsed since Emma had assumed her sole reign over Čonak.

In this unfortunate situation, it was decided within the family that my grandfather Moriz, who was now a skilled bookkeeper but could still not find work in Vienna, would be sent to Čonak as an administrator. As her son-in-law, he was family, yet not a blood relative, and might just have what was needed to sort out the problem. "He can make himself useful, and who knows, maybe he can persuade Emma to accept reality," said Luisella, who did not want to have anything to do with her own mother and therefore preferred to stay with her son Franzl in Vienna. It seemed the perfect solution for everyone: she was happy not to be with her husband every day, and he had a useful new task and something to do. After a terrible riding accident in the Prater, Vienna's Hyde Park, where he had suffered a fractured skull, he often forgot names, did not know where he had left things, walked more slowly and his hand shook when he held his teacup. His Luiserl, so much younger and full of energy, constantly criticised him and was clearly irritated by his presence. This change of scenery from Vienna to Čonak, was welcomed by both.

Moriz knew his mother-in-law, who was 11 years older than him, well enough to organise his new life in Čonak as pleasantly as possible. He did not move into the luxurious main house but into the much simpler management house, thus demonstrating that he did not want to live under the same roof as his mother-in-law. After all, he had come as the administrator. It also meant that he did not automatically have to have dinner with her every night. Emma was far from happy. Her son-in-law would be able to escape intimate family contact and her influence. He left her in no doubt as to what his mission was. There was only one fixed point of contact every day – the morning meeting in her office. And since Emma was prone to fall into a rage, Moriz never hung his hat on the nail behind the door but left it beside him on the desk, so he could snatch it up quickly and escape.

Moriz kept detailed records of all income and expenditure and went to great lengths to appease the Czech administration and promised to solve the tax problem. Again and again, money had to be injected because Čonak never made a profit. Experiments in agriculture and forestry failed, costing yet more money. Čonak remained the bottomless pit, as it had been from the beginning. Emma could not be influenced, and when the idea of selling Čonak came into the conversation, there was such an outburst of anger that the subject had to be dropped immediately. The conversation returned to the people who needed support, the family ties, the splendid hunting experiences, funny episodes, and all of nature's beauty. The problems were silenced once again.

Two years had passed since Emma's son, Wolf, had become the joint owner (with his sister, my grandmother) of Čonak. But he, too, could not exert any influence on his mother no matter how hard he tried to find a solution within the family or how often he consulted Moriz, 'the administrator', who was nearing the end of his tether. Finally, on the 28th December, 1926, Uncle Wolf wrote:

"We will probably have to solve many difficult problems and will often have to be silent even if we want to speak, but feelings must not prevail over reality when the situation has become so serious."

Inevitably the day approached when reality had to be given priority. Emma was given an ultimatum: "You have to leave Čonak and return to Germany." She refused. Uncle Wolf sent telegrams, one after another, in which he repeatedly demanded her return. Of course, the whole neighbourhood knew about it since the mayor-cum-postmaster read every telegram. This went on for many months, until patience was exhausted and an ultimatum with a fixed departure day and time was presented to Emma. My poor grandfather was entrusted with this task: "On 30th

June your departure will take place. This time it is no longer a request, but an order!"

It was seven o'clock in the morning when the coachman knocked on her bedroom door and said, "Baroness, the horses are harnessed, everything is ready for your departure." He did not receive an answer. Slightly nervous, he knocked again, louder and more insistently. Again – no answer. He went away and fetched my grandfather. Both men knocked again – still, no answer. Once more, "Emma, the carriage is ready, open the door!" Silence. Now they decided to break down the wooden door into her room.

Emma's grave in the forest.

Emma lay dressed and motionless on her bed. There was a note on the wooden bedside table saying, "I'm not leaving Čonak." An empty ampule of Veronal (rat poison) lay next to it. She had fulfilled her wish. She did not leave Čonak, and was buried in the forest across the little stream under huge oak trees at the age of 66.

≈

It was the year 1928, one year before the brief Golden Years of the global economy came to an end and Germany registered 1.4 million unemployed. The family business, rooted in agriculture and forestry with two well-managed estates, still had enough reserves to continue the 'luxury of Čonak' for the time being, pay all expenses and carry the losses.

By now Emma's daughter, Luisella, was 40 years old and couldn't wait to take over the reins of Čonak. Luckily for her, her younger brother Wolf had his hands full with the estates in Germany, which were recovering from the crisis years, so he left Čonak in her hands. Full of energy, Luisella threw herself into the task, built up a good relationship with the Czech administration and negotiated the outstanding tax payments. When the summer holidays of 1928 ended, she sent her husband, whose mission had come to an end with Emma's death, back to Vienna, where he was looked after by a servant couple in the beloved apartment at Rennweg 6 with his now 17-year-old son, Franzl. Happy days for father and son. Only in the autumn, during the deer rutting season, were the men of the family welcomed back to Čonak once again.

"A world without men would be boring," declared my grandmother generously, adding the caveat "but all men are stupid" without drawing breath.

The influence of the new Baroness, referred to by the locals both as the Baronesa and the *Panika*, extended equally across the entire region, and across all levels in the community. One of her favourite pastimes was to indulge the local children with gestures of generosity which played out like this: when the Baroness was driven in her carriage through the neighbouring villages with her yapping terrier Chimmy, she threw coins into the open hands of the children who were standing by the roadside admiring the horses and carriage. At these moments she felt like an Empress. Her smile with her immaculate teeth, and her regal posture all added to the spectacle. She was able to buy popularity and good will and would some years later be rewarded for it. Obviously, she was trying to buy love.

But she also manifested an entirely different and more intimate relationship with the locals. When dangerous potholes in the road below Čonak had to be repaired, she abandoned her guests, went down to the main road and joined the road workers in their arduous task. Like a peasant, she tied a scarf around her head, tied an apron around her waist and went down on her knees, cutting stones into shape and filling the holes. Not that they showed her how to do it, it was the Baroness who decided how it had to be done. In one word, she was omnipresent.

As the *Panika*, she wanted to know everything and interfere in everything. Intruding in the most intimate areas, she demanded to be informed in detail. The lives of her employees became part of her own life.

She gave advice, cured illnesses and shaped lives. She arranged the marriage of her long-time maid Pepi to the son of one of her employees. Without knocking on the door, she entered the rooms of her staff, disregarding any right to privacy. She did not tolerate any secrets and those who dared to have them were punished. The members of staff were part belongings, part family. If one of them fell ill, she would sit at their bedside with medication and practical advice. With her extensive medicine chest at hand she was far more useful than the far-away village doctor.

Just as she ruled over her estate, she ruled as a sovereign over her own family. When her husband had fallen from his horse and was left lying unconscious on the road with a fractured skull, she did not allow anyone to administer first-aid until she had arrived. The subsequent accusations by doctors and family that this was a gross mistake were dismissed as ridiculous.

Needless to say, Franzl, her only child, belonged to her. She did not allow him to learn Hungarian, a language she could not speak, because he could have had a 'secret language' with his father. After he completed high school, she forced him to study agriculture, which she made attractive with a huge promise: "Once you finish your studies, I will hand you over Čonak." For my hunting-obsessed father, it was an irresistible offer – like dangling a carrot in front of a horse. And to make sure that he would not lose interest in shooting while studying, she always sent him a telegram to Vienna when fresh bear-tracks were discovered on the ground. My father would then immediately drop his pencil, shut his books, and jump on the next train bound for Munkács. Eight hours later, his rifle shouldered, he would follow the bear tracks. Bear hunting was the ultimate excitement in his life.

When my father did not respond to one of the telegrams and did not go straight to Čonak but preferred to stay in Vienna, his mother rightly guessed that only a woman could be behind such unusual behaviour. She did not like this at all. "At the next opportunity, I'll confront Franzl and find out what's going on." Even as an absent mother, she had her son's life fully under control: as a student, he lived at home, quite feudally with servants, financially dependent on his mother, just as she liked it. In her head and heart, she had painted a common future for both of them in Čonak, he being the manager, she being the landowner; he being obedient, and she giving orders. She had it all perfectly worked out. Her sickly old husband, his purpose as a father and administrator fulfilled, was no longer needed and therefore pensioned off to a Hungarian friend who lived in Völsövany, about 400 kilometres from Čonak. What a practical solution for two old friends sharing life and memories from now on. Never mind that my grandfather would have been perfectly happy to go on living in Vienna with his son. But – this did not fit the master plan: "Moriz is already completely senile and useless, he would only disturb your studies," was the irrefutable explanation, in order to further eliminate any possible influence the father might have on her beloved Franzl. But that her master plan was soon to be thwarted by a woman never crossed her mind – but it happened. Her young son fell head-over-heels in love with my mother, Maria von Puchberger. Game over. The power of the purse strings could only delay the marriage till he graduated from university.

In 1934, without much fanfare, my parents had a small wedding in Budapest – only family and witnesses were invited. His mother's shadow loomed large over the occasion, giving it a sombre mood. The dress code was certainly not wedding-like: my father, whose nickname was *blue shirt*, wore a blue shirt with a dark blue suit; my mother, not a 'white' bride, chose an elegant grey suit with a small chic hat, and lilies for her bridal bouquet. Through her marriage, my Austrian mother became a Hungarian citizen.

My parents chose an exotic honeymoon destination in the mountains: Garmisch-Partenkirchen in Germany. Skiing at that time was an exclusive sport and neither of them had skied before. My father had some experience through hiking on long skis through the snow in Čonak chasing foxes, wild boar and deer. Young, fit and healthy with luck on their side they survived endless falls on dangerous runs and returned unharmed to Rennweg 6 in Vienna, where Luisella, the new mother-in-law, was already waiting impatiently.

The honeymoon was clearly over when my father was confronted by his mother: "I've changed my mind – you will not get Čonak, you will just have to find a job." It was as if the blade of a guillotine had struck him. His beloved mother had shattered his life-long dream and thrown his future into turmoil. No explanation, no justification, just a cold stare with her piercing grey-blue eyes delivering the 'death sentence' to the newly wedded couple.

One day later she left for Čonak.

Finding a job was not that easy in the Vienna of 1935, where over half a million people, or 25 per cent of the population, were now unemployed. How would my father, Hungarian on paper and therefore a foreigner, a farmer, a Baron in socialist Vienna be able to find a job? Only good contacts could help in this most difficult situation. Eventually he got a job as an accountant in a mill near Vienna. "This was our salvation – because I wasted no more time on the dream of managing Čonak. Instead, I laid the foundation for my professional life," he reflected in later years.

For the time being, the Rennweg apartment remained the young couple's home. My father endured the long daily commute to the outskirts of Vienna with patience. The newlyweds adapted to the realities of life. Luisella hardly visited Vienna, which made sharing the apartment quite easy. Not even at Christmas 1935, which would have been the first Christmas with her married son, would she leave Čonak. She chose to stay alone in the snowed-under house in the Carpathian Mountains. Again, wilderness triumphed over civilisation. I am guessing that a whiff of nostalgia captured Luisella when she ordered her ailing husband to join her in Čonak. What sort of time did they spend together? We will never know…

On 1st January, 1936, my father received a telegram in Vienna: "Your father died last night."

My newly married parents.

A day in Čonak

*You know your neighbour's face,
but not their heart*

❋

Life at Čonak was dictated by shooting – not by work, not by television, not by the stock market. In Čonak, people were focused on the animals. Anyone who wanted to sleep-in in the mornings in the mountains, in the fresh air, was disappointed. Breakfast was served between 8 and 8.30am. To be comfortable and still sleepy in a dressing gown was not allowed; one had to be shaved and properly dressed. My grandmother always got up at seven o'clock. An hour before her, the maid, called the *Dreckspatz* (another nickname, which literally means 'dirt sparrow') got up. The girl had to carry hot water into the rooms and in the winter had to get up at five o'clock to heat the stoves before the guests rose. In addition, there was the cook, *Haifa*, who had been trained as a young girl by my great-grandmother, Emma. She cooked wonderfully and imaginatively, which was appreciated by all the guests. Her day always began at six o'clock. The housemaids never wore shoes because walking barefoot was the norm, with the soles of their feet becoming as hard as leather. Some guests shuddered at this, but that did not worry my grandmother. She made sure that their hand-embroidered uniforms, with aprons, were ironed and clean. *Haifa* and the *Dreckspatz* were the only employees who slept in the kitchen house, close to the main house.

Luisella inspected the cellar and the pantry every day because there was no fridge or freezer in the Carpathians. The meals were prepared according to the seasons. After completion of the inspection, the menu was set for the day. Game was prepared in various ways according to the season; trout and crabs were caught fresh in the stream nearby. There were berries and

Haifa, the cook.

mushrooms in abundance, and if guests wanted to be popular, they would go into the forest instead of having an afternoon nap to pick berries and search for mushrooms. What couldn't be kept fresh was salted or dried. Bread, butter and cheese were home-made, which meant that life without a refrigerator was no problem. Only my grandmother's frugality spoiled the menu when she served game that had clearly gone off. In Munkács there was already a Meindl, a famous Austrian delicatessen which still flourishes in Vienna today. My grandmother bought 'little luxuries' there, but always the cheapest wine, which disappointed my parents because they would have appreciated a good wine to match the good food.

On my mother's first visit to Čonak, she met 'His Lordship', a big white Angora cat. At breakfast he would jump from Luisella's lap onto the table and walk arrogantly between plates and cups. Depending on his mood, he licked the butter or snatched a piece of sausage. I am amazed at this outlandish behaviour from my otherwise so etiquette-observing grandmother. Although I love cats, I think this was going too far.

A clear statement showed who was the boss in the house – quietly enjoying shocking her guests. "I can do what I want. If you don't like it, you don't have to come again." My mother was speechless watching this performance with 'His Lordship' ostentatiously sipping tea from Luisella's cup. Within two days my mother developed an allergic reaction and gave up on any future breakfasts, making various excuses. My father, of course, had long been immune to any bacteria and found the spectacle with the cat quite amusing.

Of course, Luisella's pets were all male. Once she found little orphaned wolves in the forest, which she proudly hand-raised like babies with a

Dreckspatz, the maid.

bottle. Only when their hunting instincts kicked in and the first chicken disappeared from the kitchen garden did she return the wolves to nature, heavy hearted.

Luisella was a supreme housewife. Before each meal, she checked that the table was properly laid – she had trained her staff to perfection – because as the hostess, she would never get up during a meal. If something went wrong, there was a huge 'drama' in the kitchen afterwards.

Lunch was always served at exactly 12.30. There was a white tablecloth, silver cutlery and Gmundner ceramics (traditional white Austrian ceramics with designs of deer in green). There were always three courses: soup, meat or fish, dessert. Coffee, with cigars and cigarettes, was served in the drawing room or, during the summer months, on the terrace. My mother was usually the only non-smoker, engulfed in a haze of smoke, which resulted in a sore throat whenever she stayed at Čonak. When I think about it, I feel that on the one hand all her visits would have been hell. On the other hand, judging by her enthusiastic accounts of the local people, of the magnificent unspoilt scenery, and above all, of stalking with her beloved husband, these all made up for the physical discomfort.

After lunch, at around two o'clock, the 'Royal Command' was spoken, when, tired or not, all guests were sent off for a nap, because my grandmother had to attend to those who were waiting in her makeshift clinic. As a trained nurse, she felt it was her duty to help the injured. During the summer months her 'clinic' was in the courtyard behind the kitchen, and during the winter months in the barn next to the kitchen. The nearest doctor lived 100 kilometres away. Needless to say, there were plenty of accidents to deal with. She disinfected and cleaned filthy wounds and professionally placed a protective bandage on them. All medicines, injections, ointments, bandages and other necessities she got free from the doctor, who in turn was allowed to fish in her stream and catch crabs. There was only one downside: fish and tablets were stuffed in the same dirty coat pocket, so that all the medicines smelled of fish.

Once, my mother watched as a young woodworker lowered his trousers in the kitchen courtyard to present his penis wrapped in newspaper to my grandmother. She expertly diagnosed gonorrhoea, gave him a scolding, and sent him away after thorough cleansing. She did not talk about her patients to her guests – that was the doctor's secret.

At 4.30 in the afternoon, after the clinic, everybody met, refreshed, for afternoon tea: coffee, tea, cake, bread, butter, jam, sausage and cheese were served on the terrace. This was also the time when the shooting plans for the evening were discussed with the gamekeeper.

Bath time was always in the evening, after an evening stroll or before the hunt, which often started at three o'clock in the morning. A rubber tub that was just big enough to sit in was carried from the courtyard into each

Franzl (left) with his friend Emil (right) on a winter hunt in the mountains in Čonak.

guest's room, as required, and filled with hot water, a duty that fell to the *Dreckspatz*. And quite accidentally and innocently, my grandmother always found a reason to come into the room, just when her son, Franzl, sat naked in the tub. She seemed to regard it as her lifelong right, as a mother, to see her son's naked body. My mother wisely kept quiet about this 'family tradition'. What could she have done anyway? To complain to her husband, who did not care about his mother's habit. Or should she confront her mother-in-law, "You are not allowed into the room when Franzl is having his bath." This would have been a declaration of war. "It is what it is," my mother conformed.

Luisella (centre) with my mother and a hunter in Čonak.

A deadly encounter

You cannot wipe away your shadow,
nor run away from the wind

❁

Two months after the death of Moriz, who had been managing Čonak for four years, his widow advertised in the *Sudetendeutscher Hunting News* for a new manager, asking for letters of application with a mandatory photo. There was a huge selection – she chose the most handsome and the youngest. The applicant liked the 'sweetener' of free hunting, which my grandmother had cunningly attached to the job description. Thus, Georg Wilhelm Sacher, the young Sudeten-German son of a forester's family, became the manager of Čonak. My grandmother seemed instantly smitten by him.

To the astonishment of the other employees, Herr Sacher was put up in the main house just six months after his appointment. Pepi, the long-standing chambermaid, who had been attached to my grandmother since she was 16, had to vacate her room. And the coquettish and flirtatious behaviour of the *Panika* surprised everybody and was impossible to avoid.

I want to compare Luisella to a flower that suddenly enjoys sun and water at the same time. She simply flourished. Hiding love is difficult, especially from other women. My mother noticed it instantly. My father did not, nor did Uncle Wolf, who came to Čonak only once a year during the rutting season, when he spent most of his time stalking the game. It did not occur to him that his sister had fallen in love with the new manager.

All the employees knew about the Baroness' new love; it was only her own family who knew nothing, except of course my mother. She had immediately noticed that the two top buttons of Luisella's silk blouse were now unbuttoned and a touch of Chanel N°5 wafted around her; she had rouge on her cheeks, powder on her nose and a spring in her step. Silently

My mother with a crayfish in Čonak.

my mother hoped that the passion would sweep over both of them like a snowstorm over a field, and that Herr Sacher would disappear at some point, so that by the time of the next deer-rutting season, the romance would be over.

My father remained unaware of the situation. In the first place, he was much more interested in the game shoot than in wasting his thoughts on 'women's business'. He found it normal that his mother, after Moriz's death, should spend most of her time in the Carpathians and that she needed someone to help her make a profit from Čonak at last. So – all was well.

As I have already mentioned, the main house in Čonak was spacious and practical, with a large sunny terrace that surrounded the living areas – the drawing room, dining room and study. Because there was no basement, keeping the house warm in winter was a particularly challenging task for the employees. There was neither electricity nor running water, no such luxury. On the first floor, where all the bedrooms were, there was only one lavatory, for everybody to share.

It was the shooting season in the autumn of 1936 when my newly married parents visited next. At the age of 47, my grandmother was a relatively young widow. In those days, widows were expected to wear black for a year, in order to display their grief and mourning. My grandmother ignored this social etiquette with the words, "Oh, *Kindchen*, that's totally unnecessary, I am not going to do that." Her husband was dead, and she blossomed with newly found vitality and a hunger for life.

During her first night in Čonak my mother had to go to the lavatory at two o'clock in the morning, a time my mother would always remember. She walked on tiptoe so the creaking floorboards under her feet wouldn't wake the others. And as the devil would have it, she ran straight into the arms of her mother-in-law, who, in her transparent nightgown, her hair dishevelled and carrying a candle, was coming from the room of the newly appointed manager. Looking away quickly and pretending not to have seen her was out of the question. The hallway was too narrow, the encounter was too real. It was a classic case of caught *in flagrante*. In the candlelight, my grandmother shot so menacing a look at my mother that she would never forget it. As if struck by lightning, she continued on her way to the lavatory, her knees buckling under her. On this disastrous night, my mother became the innocent victim of her mother-in-law's hostility.

During the following sleepless hours, her thoughts went round, and round: should I wake Franzl and tell him what I have just witnessed? Shall I let him sleep and tell him everything in the morning? Or shall I say nothing? She chose the latter. The shock of discovering that his beloved and respected mother was lying in bed with the manager, who was two years younger than he was himself, would have been too cruel.

Perhaps he would not believe it, and even naively ask his mother, "Did you really step out of the manager's bedroom last night?" Even if he hadn't said anything, his sudden awkward behaviour would have given him away at breakfast and my grandmother would immediately have guessed the reason. With all these considerations in mind, my mother's decision to keep silent was made.

Lunch break with the hunting guests (Luisella is in the white blouse).

Since they had just arrived, 'His Lordship' now offered a pleasant distraction for my mother, who felt obliged to put in an appearance at breakfast. She did not dare to look up from her plate, she was so afraid of her mother-in-law's deadly stare. On no account did she want to be alone with her in a room, so she accompanied Franzl daily into the forest to shoot game and could not wait for the departure day to arrive. My father did not notice anything. For the first time, my mother drove away from Čonak without the usual sadness, but with the utmost relief.

Luisella on the homemade bobsleigh.

Frau Luisella Sacher

Happiness – a moving cloud

A year later, when it was shooting season again, Luisella decided to get her driving licence in Munkács and bought a Tatra, a famous Czech-made car of the time. She wanted to be modern and independent. Unfortunately, she was a very fast and very bad driver, and started to insist on picking up her guests from Munkács railway station. My mother went along with her to pick up Uncle Wolf.

On the way home, driving too fast as usual, my grandmother suddenly had to hit the brakes because there were cows crossing the road. The squeal of brakes, a crash, a brief outcry – the Tatra skidded sideways, rolled over and landed on its roof in a ditch. In spite of having no seatbelts – at that time they did not exist – all three remained uninjured and scrambled out through the car's windows. Standing beside the car, which they had managed to put back on its wheels, and assessing the damage, one of them carefully tried to open a door. It opened easily. Now they all broke into loud laughter and continued on their way. A guardian angel was definitely involved.

Uncle Wolf never got on with his big sister, so he came to Čonak only once a year for the pleasure of shooting. As I have mentioned, he left the administration of the property to her, since collaboration would have been difficult. His mother Emma's emotional relationship to this property was still on his mind and he was smart enough to limit his control to the financial side of things. He moaned and groaned repeatedly because Čonak just used up money and he was left paying the bills. Making a profit from the shoot, from agriculture or from forestry simply would never happen.

When his sister introduced him to the manager, who was meant to be 'Mr Fixit', he had his doubts. "Well, you just have to let Luisella do as she thinks," he said quietly to himself, and went shooting.

It was autumn 1938 when Uncle Wolf spent a few days with Hermann, the gamekeeper, in one of the five hunting huts. In the evening, with Schnapps and a hearty snack in front of the warm fire, Hermann's tongue became looser and looser, and he could no longer restrain himself from letting the cat out of the bag: Georg Wilhelm Sacher, the 24-year-old Sudeten-German forester, who had apparently applied quite innocently for the advertised position of manager at Čonak, might have had another agenda in mind, as Hermann now explained.

He overheard him boasting in the courtyard, "I'll pick up a rich old woman, then I'll travel the world and enjoy myself!" All present guessed what this meant. A few weeks passed before Hermann's wife brought the latest gossip from the main house to her husband: the ever-diligent *Dreckspatz* had discovered some white hair on Herr Sacher's pillow. They could only belong to the Baronesa, as she was known by the locals. With this coup, the *Dreckspatz* had run to *Haifa* in the kitchen, who in turn hurried off to Hermann's wife, and so the scandal travelled like wildfire through the whole estate, because there had never been such a sensation in the area: the Baronesa, the *Panika*, was sleeping with the recently appointed brash young manager. What had hitherto been rumoured was now confirmed.

Uncle Wolf was speechless. Scandalous! Unacceptable! His sister's behaviour was totally outrageous. Not only that, as the Lady of the Manor, you never enter into an intimate relationship with employees because you have a certain status to preserve. Besides, Herr Sacher was 25 years younger than she was. "To be the source of such rumours about the family is shocking beyond belief. I have to do something. But what do I say to Luisella, who always has an argument for everything? And we have never talked about such a delicate matter." It wasn't just the following evenings, but the rest of the shooting season that were ruined for him.

And because one did not like to talk about personal matters at all, Uncle Wolf kept all this to himself and considered his next move. To write a letter – that was the answer. Back in Saxony, Uncle Wolf sat down at his big mahogany desk and wrote:

> *"Dear Luisella.*
>
> *I regretfully came to realise during my last visit that your behaviour is unacceptable to our family, and I ask you to dismiss the newly appointed manager, Georg Sacher, on the spot. I cannot allow you to bring our family into such disrepute and to make us the laughing stock of the local population and of our employees.*
>
> *In anticipation of your early reply,*
> *I remain your faithful brother,*
>
> *Wolf"*

My grandmother raged with anger as she read her brother's letter. "What impudence! I'm not going to allow him to tell me what I can or cannot do. If he thinks he can make rules for me, then he's wrong." In a letter of reply she wrote:

> *"Dear Wolf.*
>
> *If my behaviour does not suit you, then you must take note that I will not dismiss the manager, but rather I will marry him.*
>
> *I hope this decision makes you happy.*
> *I remain your faithful sister,*
>
> *Luisella"*

With this bombshell, she ruined the family and broke my father's heart. His beloved mother, the wolf mother, the symbol of demonic powers, who guarded and protected her brood, had betrayed him, abandoned him.

"You will see, my mother is a fabulous woman," he had gloated to his future wife at their first rendezvous. Back then he was the beloved son who did everything his mother wanted and would soon inherit a splendid estate. And now his mother wanted to marry a man who was two years younger than he was. In addition, this man came from a completely different milieu at a time when society was clearly divided into classes. With this blow, his admiration turned into disdain and bitter disappointment. Was he suddenly supposed to accept this man as his stepfather? This was a totally unrealistic request, expecting that motherly love is granted for life.

Still, Luisella Emma Christina von Schönberg, widowed Baroness von Ditfurth, chose to become Frau Luisella Sacher. On 4th February, 1939, she married her manager, 25 years her junior, at a registry office in

This is the only picture of Georg Wilhelm Sacher.

Uzhgorod. The witnesses were the office clerks. There were no guests. There are no wedding photos – no records at all.

She did not send out wedding announcements but wrote letters to her friends with the PS: "It's nice to have someone young in the house again." I found only a few photos of Georg Sacher, mostly of when he was still working as a manager on the estate, mingling with other hunting guests. In any case, had there been any striking photographs of Georg Sacher, my father would surely have destroyed them.

I imagine that my grandmother wore a grey suit for her wedding, the silk blouse coquettishly unbuttoned, and her handmade leather shoes, now with a higher heel to better match her husband's height. A little rouge on her cheeks but no lipstick, for in her eyes that was the prerogative of whores. A whiff of Chanel N°5 would surely not be missing. Her greying hair would be carefully arranged (she rarely went to the hairdresser). Maybe she had a flower in her hair – no, now my imagination is running away with me; she would have corrected me immediately, "*Kindchen*, what nonsense are you thinking." No, it would not have suited her. The pearls in her ears and around her neck were *de rigeur*. As a wedding gift, her 'toy boy' received a gold Omega watch. Did he give her a wedding present? No idea – wasn't his young body the ultimate gift? My parents did not buy a wedding present for them. That would have been too much hypocrisy, like giving a reward for the greatest betrayal.

It is hard to believe, but their honeymoon took them to Vienna – to a completely different Vienna from that which she remembered. Since the *Anschluss* (13th March 1938) nearly a year had passed, Austria had become the Ostmark, and instead of driving on the left, they now drove on the right. This was achieved without any accidents and with total German efficiency over one weekend. The consequences of the *Kristallnacht* – the Night of Broken Glass, as it is usually referred to in English, in November 1938, when about 95 synagogues were destroyed – had changed the multicultural, harmonious metropolis forever.

Luisella Sacher could only show her young husband the new Vienna, in which now, instead of elegant Viennese walking the streets, the Hitler Youth with rifles, shouting, "A nation helps itself," dominated the street scene. The casual life of the coffee houses was subdued; their old friends welcomed them behind closed doors in their homes. But how could they suddenly connect with the young unsophisticated manager, when they still remembered her charming husband. I imagine the stilted conversations with him: apart from the subjects of Čonak, hunting and forestry, Hitler and the looming war, there would have been nothing else to talk about.

But Luisella, nicknamed Luisa by her new husband, lacked any sensitivity to this situation. "*Nee*, Georg is quite all right and I can present him anywhere." She had clothed him elegantly in a suit and tie for their visit. With great pride, she walked on the arm of her young husband into the salons of all her friends in Vienna. Surely there was a lot of shaking of heads behind their backs.

When now, two generations later, I look at the flip side of the coin, I find it sad that no one in her family showed any understanding for the great love of her life. But by taking this bold step, outside every convention of the time, she had simply broken too many established taboos. Even today, any son would find it difficult to cope with a mother marrying someone younger than himself. I wonder how Georg Sacher felt in his new world?

My grandmother had the courage to ignore all the social norms of her time. But was it really courage, not just an irresistible sexual attraction that took hold of her? My theory is that she was jealous of her daughter-in-law, who had snatched away her beloved son when he was just a 23-year-old youngster.

It was what it was; my grandmother had made her decision, sacrificing her own family, never to be reconciled. Georg Sacher was the new man in her life who could do no wrong. But somehow, I think, Luisella must have felt awkward when she, the grey-haired widow, entered the Magistrate's office with this young man, who could have been her son. But on the other hand, she might have felt to be the lucky bride who had finally found the man of her dreams.

In 1939 the world was on the brink of collapse, while for Luisella, life at its best, had just started. There was a positive political surprise for the Sacher couple. On 23rd August, 1939, Molotov (Russia's Foreign Minister) signed a non-aggression pact in Moscow with Ribbentrop (the Molotov-Ribbentrop Pact), which meant that their life together in the Carpathians was secured for the time being. Did Georg Sacher actually enjoy his new life with the older Baroness, secretly thinking, "When the War is over, I'm going to leave her and make a good life for myself," as he had bragged a few years ago in the courtyard in front of the hunters. Could the luxurious lifestyle make him forget the realities of life?

"A simple, good-natured boy who was totally overpowered by *Die Alte*," were my mother's comments, while my father could not touch the subject of 'Herr Sacher'. Of course, I was much too young to be able to talk frankly about anything with my grandmother, which she would have not wanted anyway. Her generation did not talk about emotions, which were hidden under layers of decorum and prejudice.

Luisella had her own laws and judged the world according to her standards. She was daring: today you might say she was 'supercool', but a century ago it was completely inconceivable that a lady would entertain guests from her bed – unless of course she was 'a Royal,' or in hospital. But when my mother went on a shopping trip to Budapest, Luisella decided to entertain her for breakfast in her bedroom in the best hotel in town, where she was staying with her young husband. With flowing hair, wearing a silk nightgown, draped loosely around her shoulders, with the scent of Chanel N°5 in the air, she sat up in bed, next to her young inhibited husband who was clad in pyjamas. They drank coffee and chatted about trivial matters. My mother, almost as inhibited as 'the boy', drank her coffee as quickly as she could, devoured her croissant, and fled the awkward situation. This unusual behaviour has more to do with the unconscious than with a clear mind. In competition with my mother, Luisella demonstrated the *Ätsch*-factor (one-upmanship): "Look, what you can do, I can do even better; you stole my son from me, so I got myself an even younger man."

My grandmother at the height of her powers, in her forties.

Čonak became elegant

*The evil spirits will seek out those
who have had too many wishes fulfilled*

The new young 'Lord' of Čonak had his own ideas of style. The local maids in their bare feet were not good enough anymore and were sent home. He had hired trained staff from Budapest. They wore little black dresses with little white aprons, white hats, shoes and socks. They looked like the waitresses from *Demel* (the most traditional coffee house in Vienna). But this was Georg Sacher's idea of elegance. No one, except *Haifa* the miracle cook, walked barefoot. His wife, Luisella, did not object: she paid the higher salaries and trained the new staff. The local newspaper, cut up into squares, had served for toilet paper until now. To the delight of my parents, it was replaced with proper toilet paper. Better wine was served with dinner, and gamey deer meat disappeared from the menu. In addition, 'His Lordship' the white cat, who had walked cheerfully on top of the table, was banished under the table. He snarled every time Herr Sacher came near him. Finally, some of the armchairs that had been ripped by bayonets during the Bolshevik time were freshly upholstered. In short, a touch of luxury pervaded Čonak.

The new 'Lord' of Čonak, invited his friends to hunt. Luisella often joined in, even though she herself never took a gun into her hand. Was it her great love of animals that kept her from shooting them? I guess, that was one reason. Also, hunting was very much a sport for men only. In any case she did everything to make her young man feel comfortable in her house. This also meant that the family had to accept him. Instead of my father, Georg now sat at the head of the dining table.

What a change! Just a short time ago he had been an employee who had to make an appointment before each visit to the Baroness, and now he was the landlord. That's some mighty career jump. Of course, he was not accustomed to eating with heavy silver cutlery, and he did not know how to hold knife and fork *comme il fault*. When the maid came to him with the large serving-bowl, small beads of sweat formed on his forehead, because a meal without spilling anything was always a stressful challenge. His lack of table manners disturbed my mother more than my father, who had a much bigger problem with his stepfather: this was the *'du'* word (meaning 'you'), the informal way of addressing somebody, like *tu* in French. My father did not want to and could not bring himself to say *du* to this man who could not even speak proper High German, the language of all educated Austrians. Every bone in his body rebelled; just thinking about it made it impossible to get the word out of his mouth. Principled as he was, my father continued to say *sie*, the formal and polite form.

My grandmother, tight lipped, repeatedly overheard *sie*, until she could no longer stand it and confronted my father: "It is not at all acceptable that you continue to address my husband with *sie*. I am asking you for the last time to address him with *du*." My father refused. It was the first and only time in his life that he openly confronted and disobeyed his mother. Those two letters broke the bond between mother and son forever. In spite of great tragedy later in life, the rift could never be mended.

My father showed his stepfather that he neither accepted him as a family member nor placed him on the same social level. Georg Sacher remained the manager, my father the young Baron. Among aristocrats, it is customary for men to address other men and for women to address other women automatically with *du* at the first meeting, which affirms that one 'is speaking the same language'. But between a man and a woman, *sie* would be used. My mother would have said *sie* to my father's best friend all her life.

By using *sie* to his stepfather, my father made a clear stand and snubbed his mother: two fingers to her choice of second husband.

Other family members faced the same dilemma: Uncle Wolf swallowed his pride for the sake of peace in the family and was persuaded to say *du*, which made him look good in the eyes of his sister, while my father lost an ally. For all the established long-serving families and employees this new situation with the young manager suddenly becoming the boss, giving orders and throwing his weight around, it was an embarrassing situation to which my grandmother turned a blind eye. He was now the most important person in her life. The ear and the heart of the mistress of Čonak belonged to him alone. Did the employees lose their respect for the *Panika*? I suspect so.

≈

Until the non-aggression pact with Russia ended in June 1941, the Ukraine had been under Nazi German civil administration. This meant that the so-called grain store of the East was shamelessly plundered as food supply for Germans, while the local population died of hunger.

Thanks to the well managed agriculture in Čonak there was enough food for everybody. As politically secured German citizens, the course of the War seemed to be favourable to the Sacher couple. For now the young and healthy landlord was safe from the long arm of Hitler's recruiting drive. But for how long? As the War against Russia proved disastrous with the number of dead soldiers growing daily, Georg Sacher's chance of being overlooked diminished by the day.

A similar situation had spared my father, as he was a Hungarian who lived in Austria. The downside for him was that as a 'foreign Austrian', he had the greatest difficulty finding a job. Still, that was better than being shot as a conscript in the War. In that sense, my father was lucky.

After the argument about the *du* word, my parents only visited Čonak once more – a final visit to say good-bye. It was the year 1943 and Georg Sacher was no longer present, having been conscripted into the army. My parents came with their two-year-old son, my brother Nikolaus. When they arrived, *Haifa*, the old cook, now toothless and wrinkled, joyfully kissed his little hand. She still cooked superbly and was thus cooking for the fourth generation of the family.

Heavy hearted, my father trudged through the autumn foliage from hut to hut, spending one last night in each hut accompanied by Hermann, the master of the shoot. But his thoughts were no longer on shooting and hunting. With his Leica camera, he photographed the beloved mountains for one last time and produced a series of black-and-white photos, a unique panoramic image of Čonak. It was copied and framed and hung in almost every room of our apartment. It was as though he wanted to hang on to it and never let go. I have one of those pictures too, of course.

Meanwhile my mother, with great pride, showed off her son, with *Haifa* never leaving their side. Out of thick white lambswool she had knitted a Rusnak outfit for him and complete with a hat he did look just like a little Rusnak. He was endlessly kissed and caressed. Again and again tears flowed, and saying good-bye was heart wrenching. Everyone knew that there was to be no reunion. Only my grandmother remained optimistic and ignored the political warning signs.

Although the death penalty was in force for illegal possession of weapons, my father could not separate himself from two beloved guns, one of which he named the 'thunderbolt of the Carpathians'. "The stupid Nazis," – he had no respect for them at all – "they'll never find it." He dismantled his guns, lubricated them, wrapped them in a lot of newspaper and packed them in two wooden crates. He did not even have an answer ready in the eventuality that he might be caught – so daring.

He was right, both rifles survived undetected, and when the War ended, he was lucky enough to sell them to good friends, equally keen

My brother, Nikolaus, dressed like a little Rusnak.

hunters who did not dare to keep their rifles. With the proceeds we were able to buy a discarded Jeep from the American Army and so the family became mobile again.

My grandmother's sole reign in Čonak started after the death of her mother Emma, and lasted for 10 years. She could not wait to take over the running of the estate and had gladly left the spacious apartment in Vienna to her now married son. As life in Vienna, as in all major cities, became more and more difficult, my father lost his job. The aristocratic network came to the rescue again: Baron Bachofen von Echt owned the Murstätten Estate in the state of Styria and needed a trusted manager. It was the first and only time that my father's study of agriculture was useful. We all had plenty of food and my father ran rings around the Nazi inspectors. Being a wine country, and not knowing if one was alive the next day, made the wine flow freely. It was the only time in my parents lives that alcohol was part of their daily diet. Since the Hitler regime granted all sorts of privileges to farm owners because they were essential in 'feeding the nation', it meant that life was good for all of us during the War.

I was born in this house in Lebring. My mother and brother are at the gate.

I was born in Lebring on a Sunday morning on my mother's birthday, 15th April, 1943, in my parents' bed. We lived in a cosy farmhouse on the estate, which had its own small garden with lots of apple trees.

My birth was a good reason for my grandmother to leave Čonak for a few days and come and 'inspect' her second grandchild. However, during these turbulent times the War was the number one topic. There were many discussions with political debates dominating the evenings, although *Die Alte*, despite the precarious situation, was determined to return to the Carpathians, pack up some family treasures from the now locked up flat in Vienna, and send them in a container to Čonak.

When my father expressed grave doubts about this decision, she said, "*Ach*, Franzl, in the Carpathians it is just as safe as in Vienna or Frankfurt, because if the Russians cross the Carpathian Mountains, all of Europe will be lost anyway." Any further arguments she did not want to hear. Jewellery (including the diamond earrings of Anna Constantia von Cosel), securities and cash went to the bank in Munkács. This bank was as safe as any bank in Frankfurt — was her opinion. My parents were silenced. My father had to watch as his inheritance was laid at the feet of the Russians: "She always knows better — what can I do."

And so, my grandmother's first and last visit to Lebring resembled a *Götterdämmerung*. "I knew I would not see *Die Alte* again for a long, long time," but no tears were wasted on her. Why should there be tears? She had rejected every well-meant piece of advice and it would be 12 years before we would see her again.

Already, truth and history were being suppressed: a few years later, on 23rd February, 1947, she wrote a letter in English from Čonak: *"I had seen it all coming since 1938"*. Such a distortion of the actual facts was irritating and hurtful.

In March, 1944, the German Army invaded the Western Carpathians and one million Jews were murdered in the Ukraine. The entire Jewish population was 'cleansed' by July of the same year. Only 20 per cent of Jews survived the concentration camps. It was self-evident to my grandmother that she should offer shelter to the local Jewish families and save their lives.

Shortly thereafter, the German Army was forced to withdraw; many villages had been intentionally destroyed, which in 1945 resulted in about 10 million homeless people. The Red Army was on the march. Around this time, the Sudeten-German hunter families of Čonak decided to leave the

Carpathians. They could not persuade my grandmother to come along. Already in September 1944 our only Austrian neighbour, Count Georg von Schönborn-Buchheim, had decided to leave his beloved Beregvar and save what could be saved. But my grandmother stayed. Again, she knew better.

So, with her Pepi, who was now married and had nowhere else to go, the native farm hands and her animals, she waited for a favourable end to the War and for her young husband to return from the Front.

In the isolation of Čonak, the reality of the atrocities of the War almost passed her by without a trace. Six-and-a-half million people died because of the War. But Luisella Sacher naively believed that her life in Čonak would go on forever.

My brother and I as infants.

The Russians are coming

*You can plan for the future
– but not for the past*

✻

The Russian invasion was no surprise. My parents had prophesied it a year before, when my grandmother was visiting Lebring. But at the time she had replied with conviction, "*Kindchen*, if that happens, then all of Europe is lost – no, this will never happen."

Even Uncle Wolf was realistic enough to write off the beloved property. In spring 1944, he sold his 50 per cent share to a Berlin forestry company, which in a barter deal gave him some apartment houses in Berlin. This was, in principle, a smart move, especially for family reasons, as cooperation with his young brother-in-law and his sister would have become more and more problematic. The fact that those houses were in Berlin, which was later to be East Germany, was bad luck.

Just as before World War I, when Emma would not leave Čonak as the Partisans crossed the Carpathian mountain range, her daughter Luisella also ignored the rumours of Russian soldiers appearing sporadically out of the blue asking for food and lodging, intimidating the frightened farmers. She thought these stories simply ridiculous, spun by the superstitious Rusnaks, just as her mother Emma had, even though her very personal idyll had already been considerably disturbed when her Sudeten-German husband was called up to join the Eastern Front in a last attempt at victory. As a healthy not-yet-30-year-old, he had no hope of being overlooked. Herr Sacher was made a Sergeant in Tank Division V, Budapest Army Division.

When the conscription papers arrived at the house demanding his immediate departure, Luisella chauffeured him to Budapest. They drove in the new dark green Tatra, which she had given him for their first wedding anniversary. Yes, for her young husband, the wallet was always open – what would my father have given to have had a motorbike as a student?

They spent one last night together at the same luxury hotel where they had received my mother a few years earlier for breakfast in bed. Luisella embraced her husband, who had reluctantly exchanged his hunting gear for a military uniform. On that last rendezvous, they made a pact: "Whatever happens, when all this is over, we'll meet in Čonak. I'll be waiting there for you." With those words still on her lips, she watched the long military transport train with her husband squeezed onto the steps slowly roll out of Budapest's main railway station towards the East. She was one of the hundreds of waving women who was seeing her man for the last time. Only she differed from the other women: she did not weep, even though her heart was broken.

Alone, she drove back home. She was sad, but belief in their reunion gave her strength; fear of the Russians was unknown to her. After all, she was the *Panika* of Čonak, in charge of everything; it was here that she belonged. Besides, she had Pepi and her animals, although the new dog could not replace beloved Chimmy, the Skye Terrier. She remembered Chimmy sitting with the coachman in the front of the carriage and barking fiercely at every street dog passing, because he wanted to make it clear that he was the boss here. Every Saturday Pepi's task was to bathe him, having played hide-and-seek through the whole house before catching him. At last, shiny and clean, he strutted proudly up and down with his tail erect. But now there were no guests, no one to parade proudly in front of, only the hope of an early end to the War and a happy end with her husband.

It was Christmas Eve, 1944. The Russians had just encircled Budapest. Outside there was a blizzard and the temperatures had plunged to -20° Celsius, but in the house it was comfortably warm with no lack of wood from the surrounding forest. Oblivious to the realities of the War, my grandmother did not know how dangerous her situation had become. She was roaming around somewhere in the house when she heard a heavy knocking at the door. She opened the door and a group of frozen, filthy, Russian soldiers surprised her. They immediately pushed her roughly aside to gain entry. The pearls around her neck and dangling from her ears were alluring – irresistible. The biggest and strongest of the group of men tore them from her, without saying a word, and put them in his dirty coat pocket. Her simple gold watch with its brown leather strap was torn off by one of the other men. Then came the order from the one with the most stars on his collar, "You have an hour, you can take your bed, bedding, a chair, cooking utensils and a spoon – and then you are OUT, because from now on the house belongs to the Russian State."

Luisella was neither hysterical nor did she cry, but thought quick-wittedly, "There is Nikolai down in the village; he is a decent fellow, has always been loyal to me. I'll go to him immediately, tell him what has happened – he'll have to take me in."

Still feeling like the *Panika* she once was, she gave a last command, harnessed the horses and loaded her bed and the few possessions allowed. Then she hurried down the shortcut behind the house through the forest into the village and knocked at Nikolai's door. Stunned, he looked at her and listened, speechless with an open-mouth: "The Russians have thrown me out of my house – I have nowhere to go. You have to take me in." It sounded more like an order than a plea. Together they trudged back to the house through the snowstorm: "I will become your farmhand – that is a promise." He knew her capacity for hard work. "I'll help in the household, in the fields, wherever you need me, but you'll have to give me a roof over

Luisella with Chimmy, the Skye Terrier.

my head." Nikolai just nodded; he had no choice. They returned to Čonak one last time to pick up the few items she was allowed to take.

Nikolai's wife was even less pleased with the unexpected houseguest. Unwillingly, she opened the wooden front door of the little house in the hope that this unwanted visitor would soon disappear.

The house was too small to accommodate another bed, so the Baroness' bed was placed in the wooden shed, which was an annex to house the pigs. The pigs had to be moved closer together and the manure was pushed to the other side of the sty, and *voilà*, the bedroom was ready. The stench and the grunting of the four pigs, which were Nikolai's wealth, hardly bothered my grandmother because she appreciated the warmth of the animals and of course a roof over her head. Within a few hours the 57-year-old landlady became a maid, who had to fit into the life of a small local farmer. The most difficult challenge was to subordinate herself to the orders of another woman, a farmer's wife. But my sharp-thinking grandmother knew that there was no way out at this moment in her life. What was going through her mind a lot was not so much her own position, but the fate of her beloved animals left in Čonak in the hands of Russian soldiers: what would happen to them?

Back in Austria, where listening to a foreign radio station was forbidden on pain of death, my parents disregarded these restrictions and secretly pressed their ears to the radio in a darkened room. The BBC reported on the advance of Russian troops and the subsequent occupation of the Carpathians. This was no surprise, it was expected. "What has happened to *Die Alte*? The Russians have surely thrown her out of the house, maybe killed her. Probably simply shot her," my father speculated. Thoughts like, "It really serves her right," did come to mind because she had dismissed all warnings of the impending danger during her last visit to Austria, when she had declared, full of conviction, "I am not running away from the Russians, because Čonak is mine and I am not scared of them," hugely overestimating herself.

The feared Red Army not only crossed the Carpathians, but also marched in full force across the border into Austria. Under Hitler, our part of the country had been renamed the Reichsgau of Styria and was easily accessible to the advancing Russian forces.

It was 29th March, 1945. What was left of the defence forces of the so-called *Volkssturm* were only able to offer sporadic resistance, and so the total collapse of Austria soon became a reality. There were stories of extreme cruelty, the plundering hordes of Russians, followed close behind by General Tito's troops with similar destructive fury. Since Styria was the closest entry point into Austria, my 'Hungarian' parents recognised the immediate danger, packed their most essential belongings in a car, and fled with our friends, the estate owners, and 100,000 others, towards the western part of Austria.

For now, our own survival took priority and left no room to worry further about *Die Alte*.

The last photograph of Luisella before she disappeared, in her fifties.

The first sign of life

*The sea does not deny
small rivers access, hence its depth*

❋

Almost a year went by before there was any sign of life from Čonak. It came through a phone call from a stranger in a refugee camp in Bad Gastein, Austria. He had news for us.

As one might expect, my grandmother did not have time for small talk, but preferred serious, meaningful conversations. She took a clear line when it came to politics: she hated Hitler and was sympathetic to the Jews. In the Carpathians, Jews and Rusnaks lived peacefully side-by-side, with 90 per cent of all Eastern Jews living in the Ukraine. Everybody had their place in society. The Rusnaks were the agricultural workers, coachmen, woodcutters and farmers, the Jews mostly craftsmen and traders, moneylenders and shopkeepers, but above all they were the 'movers and shakers' in this godforsaken corner of the Carpathians. When, for example, the telegram announcing the death of Donald, my great-grandfather, arrived at the post office in Kerecky and was read out loud by the Mayor, a Jewish boy who waited there to catch news, grabbed the sensational telegram and ran with it to Čonak to deliver it and collect a tip.

In the village of Bereznik, below Čonak, was a synagogue and an Orthodox church. The Rabbi never greeted the Schönberg family, no one knows why – did he think he was better than they were? The scruffy 'Pope', as the Head of an Orthodox Church is called, was friendly and even offered to officiate at family funerals in the absence of a Protestant church.

The difference between Jews and Rusnaks was clearly evident from the way they dressed: the Rusnaks either walked barefoot, like *Haifa* and the maids in Čonak, or had some sort of cloth wrapped around their feet instead of socks, combined with anything that could serve as a shoe. Jews on the other hand always wore shoes. The local girls had braids and mostly wore skirts with a white embroidered blouse. In contrast, the Jewish girls always wore a headscarf because they wanted to conceal their shorn heads and had no special way of dressing. Anything would do. Intermarriage was out of the question. Boys and girls further divided into separate groups. I am sure that there would have been some tragic love stories.

In terms of character, the two races were worlds apart. The Rusnaks were terribly superstitious: because poor Joshi had dandruff, which could only have come from an evil spirit, he could not marry his girlfriend. Whenever it got dark in the forest, they were overcome with panic, believing that evil spirits would drop down on them out of the crown of a tree, and would run out into the fields in order to escape. This meant that none of the local men could be employed as hunters. The burden of these superstitions crushed all progress. Ghosts ruled over logic and common sense.

During the German administration of the Ukraine, military patrols were sent out to capture Jews. My grandmother hid Jewish families in the forest of Čonak, where she knew every hut, cave and natural hiding place. As the *Panika* of her house, and without any fear of authority, she simply ordered more food to be cooked, which she then brought to her hidden friends at night. Consequently, she saved a lot of Jewish lives during the German occupation. Needless to say, the rescued families held her in high esteem.

When the Germans were defeated and expelled from the Carpathians by the Russians in 1944, the remaining resident Jews were able to live freely again. However, on a political level, there were negotiations to allow a certain quota of Jews to leave for Israel if they so wished. The resettlement was to take them first to Austria via a detention centre.

Twenty local Jews received an official exit permit. They discussed it among themselves and came to the conclusion that one person was to be left behind in order to smuggle my grandmother into the group and return the favour: they knew of her fate, of her seemingly hopeless situation as Nikolai's maid in the pigsty. With her looks, she was able to fit into the group as a Jew without any problems. By taking advantage of this possibly life-saving offer, she would be able to end her miserable existence immediately, travel comfortably by train, and arrive in Vienna within a day. The dice lay in her hands: would she rather choose freedom and find her son or stay and wait for her missing husband.

It appears that she made up her mind quickly, chose the latter, and declined, much to the astonishment of her Jewish friends. She thanked them for the kind offer and stayed put, although she had not heard from her husband for two years, which indicated that he was probably dead.

She was determined to keep her promise: "Whatever happens, I'll wait for you in Čonak." Miracles do happen – perhaps Georg would suddenly appear. What then? If she left, would she have abandoned him? No amount of logic from her Jewish friends could persuade her to leave. But at least she asked Mr Leibovitz, the leader of the group, to contact her son. At that stage, she had no idea if he was alive. With the help of the Red Cross my father was found.

The Jewish transport from the Ukraine arrived at the refugee camp in Bad Gastein at the end of 1945. By pure coincidence, we lived very close by. Our new home was Tenneck, just down the valley from Bad Gastein. As a spa with healing hot-water wells, Bad Gastein had been popular with the Austrian Jews since 1935, even before the War, offering its guests a synagogue and a hotel with kosher food. It was mostly Viennese Jews who enjoyed the fresh air and the healing springs of Bad Gastein. It seemed logical that a refugee camp should be set up there. Approximately 2,000 Jewish refugees were accommodated in five hotels and various private houses. There was plenty of work for them and good schooling for their children.

The unexpected phone call was the first sign of life from my grandmother: "We have just come from Munkács and have news from the Baroness." So, *Die Alte* is alive! Immediately, my parents got in their Jeep and drove to Bad Gastein.

Mr Leibovitz, whose long white beard impressed my mother, was about 60 years old. He welcomed my parents in a hotel lobby and introduced his wife and four children, who all owed their life to my grandmother. He said, "The Baroness

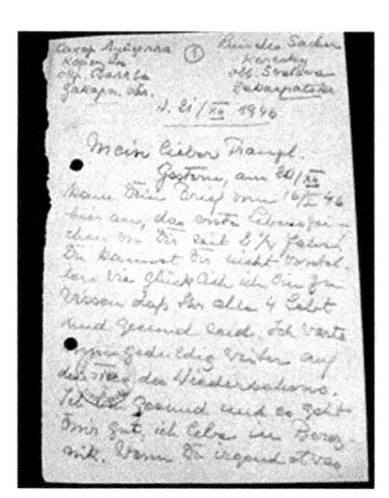

The first of many letters Luisella sent to Franzl.

was thrown out of her house by the Russians and is now living at Nikolai's place in Bereznik, in a sort of shack which is the pigsty. She is healthy, full of energy, works in the fields and leads the life of a peasant. Although she has lost all her possessions, she could not be talked into leaving. She said that her missing husband might suddenly appear, so she wanted to wait for him." Then he handed over a piece of paper with her address.

My parents looked at each other knowingly. She had always been stubborn – but why had the experience of the past years not given her a better sense of reality? They thanked Mr Leibovitz, put the note with grandmother's address in a pocket, and drove back to Tenneck.

When the camp in Bad Gastein was shut down in the spring of 1946, the Leibovitz family emigrated to America. Our paths diverged forever.

Anna Constantia, Countess von Cosel

*Words that are whispered often go further
than those that are spoken aloud*

❋

She is the most glamorous ancestor of the Schönberg family, a famous German figure who has inspired historians and novelists over centuries. I can't help but compare these two women, as Anna Constantia von Cosel was an ancestor of Luisella von Schönberg, with both their lives being marked by love, tragedy, and captivity.

She lived from 1680-1765, and became the lover of Augustus the Strong, King of Poland, Elector of Saxony. He was the *Übermensch* of his time.

As his 'Mistress to the Right', Anna Constantia was the woman with the most privileges and power. She had three children by the King, two daughters and a son, who was baptised with the name Friedrich Augustus Count von Cosel. His granddaughter married Friedrich Augustus Wolf von Schönberg, so the Cosel bloodline and that of Augustus the Strong came into our family. Although the times and circumstances were quite different, there are many parallels in the fates of both women. Were certain genes passed down to my grandmother – or was it pure coincidence?

Grandmother was always so proud of her thick bushy half-moon-shaped eyebrows, which she surely inherited from the Cosel side of the family. After her return from Russia, an eyebrow pencil was the first luxury item she bought.

Anna Constantia von Cosel, with her keen mind and physical beauty, corresponded to the ideal of a woman at the time: she had flawless white skin with a lightly powdered face, neck and décolté, enhanced with a rosy blush on her cheeks, a distinct wasp waist and pinned-up hair. Her grace

Anna Constantia von Cosel and Augustus the Strong, King of Poland.

and pride were complemented by intelligence and great vitality. Augustus the Strong, a man of impetuous power and a womaniser, fell for her hook, line and sinker.

It has been said that during a major fire in the castle at Dresden, a dramatic encounter took place between Anna and Augustus, who was alerted to the catastrophe. The all-engulfing flames were coming from Anna's living quarters. Although dressed in an evening gown and wearing jewellery, she took charge of the fire and put herself in command of the fire brigade. The King was so impressed with this strong and elegant lady that he asked her to stop fighting the flames and invited her into his carriage to whisk her away to safety.

For 100 days Anna Constantia von Cosel resisted the King's offer of becoming his mistress – she was too proud and clever to just throw herself into the arms of this lustful man. She wanted certain guarantees: first his current mistress had to make way, with the wife keeping her established place. She also demanded a monthly allowance and a secret marriage contract, which would give their relationship some longevity and meaning. 'Love makes you blind' – or in this case, 'makes you lose your mind'. The King agreed to everything, against the advice of his closest confidant, who was shocked beyond belief: "How irresponsible and selfish, he will plunge Saxony into a catastrophic situation if somehow the public finds out that the married Catholic King is a bigamist." To have a mistress was entirely acceptable to everybody but to have a secret wife was a step too far. In addition to this, Anna never left the King's side during meetings about important state affairs and even dared to express her opinion and contradict the ministers. "Such impudence! We cannot tolerate this woman interfering in our state affairs," hissed the ministers behind her back, and secretly plotted her demise.

But that was not going to be easy because she was 'superwoman': she had grown up on a country estate with two older brothers and learned to ride, shoot and drink like a man. When she went hunting, she sat confidently astride the horse rather than adhering to the customary feminine way of riding side-saddle, coyly placing both legs on one side of the horse. She could shoot better than the King's huntsmen and when the Royal hunting party was invited for a *Drinkfest*, she could drink as much as any man, and amused the King more than any of his drinking companions. She was one of the boys, but when she entered the Court in Dresden, she transformed herself into a gracious and stunning beauty. "The Countess von Cosel is here," was murmured through the corridors of the palace when she sailed through a room, clothed in exquisite robes with exotic furs and lace, and with precious jewellery embellishing her appearance.

The King could not keep his eyes off her and it is no wonder that he showered her with gifts and having bought the magnificent Pillnitz Palace, he gifted it to her.

To the horror of his ministers, the King would not be separated from her even when he went off to war in Poland. She undertook the long and arduous journey in a horse-drawn carriage and exchanged her luxurious life in the castle for the primitive war camp in Poland. The ambitious Augustus the Strong was determined to become King of Poland, which meant fighting wars, changing religion and spending a great deal of money. And again, Anna sat next to him during the strategy meetings of the war. She questioned, forced discussions and drove the generals to exasperation, at a time when war was entirely 'a man's business'.

Her feminine instinct told her that she could not leave the King alone for a minute because of his roving eye. In the years 1708 and 1709 she bore him two daughters, and three years later, a son.

Anna was exhausted after her third difficult birth and did not have the energy to undertake the arduous journey back to the war camp but opted instead to stay at Pillnitz. This was a fatal mistake. Immediately her enemies saw a chance to win the King over to a new mistress: they presented a Catholic Polish countess to him, who was politically better suited. Without delay, and so Anna could not exert any further influence on the King (she argued against his chosen path of the Poland policy), Anna Constantia von Cosel, 'Mistress to the Right', was placed under house arrest in 1713. No explanation was given. The time for revenge had come. Her flood of letters in which she explained her situation and declared her continued undying love never reached the King. Her enemies told the King that she would blackmail him with their secret marriage contract and therefore she should never be freed.

On Christmas Eve 1716, Saxon soldiers arrested her and moved her to the Stolpen Fortress.

On Christmas Eve 1944, exactly 228 years and many generations later, Russian soldiers threw Luisella von Schönberg out of her house.

Appropriately for their status, they both wore diamond and pearl earrings, which were ruthlessly pulled from their ears by their arresting soldiers.

Both women were emancipated before their time, wanted to break out of the pre-determined mould, and live as equals in a man's world; Anna wanted to shape politics, my grandmother believed she was untouchable by politics. Both could speak foreign languages, were highly educated and could legitimately claim equality with any man. Today they would be in top managerial positions. But they shared one big character flaw: they could not be told anything and listened to no one, relying entirely on their own instincts, which led them astray. They drew strength from unrealistic illusions, which helped them to survive terrible hardships. And both ladies lost their great personal fortunes in the course of their lives.

While Anna Constantia von Cosel brought every room to a standstill with her beauty and grace, my non-glamorous grandmother achieved the same with her strong personality and charisma, which, as a child, I found intimidating. She would never simply blend in amongst others in a crowd.

Anna lacked any diplomatic instinct to prevent her falling victim to the intrigues at the Court; she always found her own reasons to ignore well-intentioned advice. Her pride and her naive belief in eternal love led to her downfall: "The King will come and visit me, then I will be able to explain everything to him." That's why she stayed in the tower of the fortress, though she twice had an opportunity to escape – just as my grandmother did not seize her chance to leave. Both ladies held on to their illusions, not wanting to recognise the reality of their hopeless situations. Or would it simply have been too cowardly to just flee? Did my grandmother's pride prevent her from disappearing as a 'Jewish refugee'? Here is the irony of fate: my grandmother deposited all her jewellery, including a magnificent pair of diamond earrings inherited from Anna Constantia von Cosel, one of many tokens of love from Augustus the Strong, in a bank deposit box in Munkács. With absolute confidence, she had declared, "The bank here is just as safe as any bank in Frankfurt."

What was the fate of the earrings? I toy with the thought that they now belong to some Russian lady and have been shown off during an outing to the opera in Moscow or Vienna. Or were they simply thrown into the mud by a soldier who only wanted a gold watch and did not care for earrings?

The Stolpen Fortress, where Anna Constantia von Cosel was imprisoned for 49 years.

Thanks to her incredibly good health, Anna Constantia von Cosel survived 49 years of imprisonment in the tower at Stolpen Castle. At the beginning of her isolation she was guarded by 70 soldiers because she was considered such a political threat. In total isolation with no contact to the outside world, she held onto the belief that one day she would find justice. She made herself beautiful, combed her hair into a stylish chignon, put her old wardrobe together as well as she could so as to be elegant enough to receive the King at any time.

He did come once – to try out new cannon balls against the thick walls of the fortress. When Anna got the news that the King was there and did not come to see her, she fainted, and was sick for many days. Anna was a woman who was often afraid and shed tears into her pillows during many sleepless nights. Unlike her, *Die Alte* never cried, and declared without hesitation, "*Nee*, I was never afraid. Since I have never been beaten, why should I have been afraid? "

Anna Constantia von Cosel's 49 years of imprisonment, make my grandmother's 11 years behind the Iron Curtain seem quite brief, but Anna was living in a castle with staff, while my grandmother suffered extreme hardship. But then, *Die Alte* had a young lover in the labour camp. Who was better off? Neither woman ever lost her faith, both believing in a miracle: the King would come and visit her – Herr Sacher would suddenly reappear. Even in 1960, when he had already been missing for 15 years, my grandmother lodged a new search request with the Red Cross in Salzburg.

The 85-year-old Anna Constantia von Cosel died 32 years after the death of her beloved King, alone and forgotten in Stolpen. Her children had become strangers, the outside world unreal. No one remembered what 'crime' she had actually committed and why she was still there. But before her last breath, she determined exactly where and how she wanted to be buried.

The Stolpen Fortress was badly damaged by Napoleon, and the tomb of Anna Constantia von Cosel was lost for years. It was only in 1881 that it was rediscovered. Today a simple gravestone can be seen. My grandmother also gave clear instructions regarding her grave, which no longer exists.

From Baroness to slave

*He who has changed his clothes
has not changed his character*

Before meeting Mr Leibovitz, my parents kept asking themselves, "If *Die Alte* is still alive, where would she be living and what happened to Georg Sacher?" Of course, my parents never accepted him as her husband. A myriad of variations swarmed through their heads – only one thing was clear: the Russian occupation of the Ukraine meant that life as a landowner had definitely come to an end. And as a former capitalist, she belonged now to a new hostile class.

But what had happened to her husband, who had been conscripted sometime in 1942 and was now missing? Now that he had her address at hand, my father resumed his usual correspondence, this time with many questions. But his letters remained unanswered. The anxious wait for the daily mail slowly lessened. One day, however, when he was routinely opening the day's office mail, his mother's familiar handwriting struck him: a Russian stamp, with an additional stamp that noted 'Military Censorship Civil Mail 31 54', addressed to my father. He opened the letter in haste. On a piece of paper, which looked as if it had been torn out of an exercise book was written in pencil:

"My dear Franzl.

Yesterday, on the 20th of December 1947, your letter of 16th January 1946 arrived here. The first sign of life from you for two and a half years. You cannot imagine how happy I am to know that all four of you are alive and healthy. I am patiently waiting for the day of our reunion.

*I am healthy and I am well, I live in Bereznik. If you know anything about Georg, please write to me. I have no news from him.
Kisses and hugs to all four of you, with all my heart,
Your <u>Mother</u>"*
(Mother was underlined).

In the paranoia of the post-war period, every letter from the Soviet Union was censored. Against the backdrop of the bureaucracy of both victors in the War, one can understand how my father's first letter from Tenneck, in the American zone, to the Ukraine, now Russian, took 11 months to get there. But in the end, it did arrive. The first question, "Why did you not leave with the transport of the kind Jews?", she never answered.

How many thousands of letters were simply thrown away, perhaps because the writing was illegible or because nobody could translate the language, or because there was just nobody who cared? How many thousands of lives and hopes hung on one letter that never arrived? I wonder if there were military guidelines? My grandmother sometimes wrote in English to make it easier for the Allied censors. Postcards were a variant: there was less to read and no envelope to open, no secrets. Looking back, I can imagine the enormous effort involved: how many translators must have been employed by the occupying forces, who did nothing other than read mostly harmless, desperate letters. For the Soviets, it was important to prevent any potential negative propaganda.

So, we could only guess how *Die Alte* was really doing, because in every letter she had a standard sentence: "I'm fine and I'm healthy and I'm looking forward to our reunion." This sentence was her lure for the authorities, so they could seal the letter again and hopefully send it on quickly. No hidden secrets in her letters, just the simple desire to return to her family. In the first six letters, she always signed, "Your faithful mother", heavily underlined, so that my father would be reminded that he still had a mother, and especially that SHE was that mother. My mother told me, "At the very beginning of my marriage, it was obvious that I had to allay her jealousy and diminish her feelings of losing her only son. I told her once that she would be his mother forever, but I did not know if I would be his wife forever." Clever Mumi – which is what we called my mother.

In the subsequent flood of letters my grandmother always signed with the familiar *Die Alte*. Except for the first letter, all subsequent letters were written in pen and blue ink. As I was reading her letters, I kept wondering where she got the pen and ink from. The penny dropped, of course: from the schoolgirl in Nikolai's house. Only on Sundays was it possible to borrow pen and paper, which was carefully pulled out from the school exercise book to create her stationery. Sunday became her letter-writing day.

What a turn fate had taken.

Many years before – but it was still firmly anchored in the little girl's memory – the Baroness had driven elegantly in her horse-drawn carriage through the village as the benevolent landowner and had thrown money into her open hands when she and other children had lined the roadside admiring the passing *Panika*. These gestures of generosity made my grandmother feel powerful and loved. Not in her wildest dreams did she think that the little girl with the runny nose and dirty hands would one day become her lifeline to the outside world.

How many of the weekly letters were lost somewhere in the bureaucracy? I could imagine that her handwriting eventually become a familiar sight to the censors, who would by then no longer bother opening each letter, making life easier for themselves and speeding up the whole process. But if the translators changed frequently then the whole process was stuck in a slow grinding groove.

In addition to school times and working in the fields, daylight also dictated my grandmother's writing possibilities. There was no electric light in Nikolai's house. The family rose with the chickens in the morning and went to bed with them in the evening. Despite these obstacles, my parents received 34 letters in 1947. Almost all of them had been opened, looked at, read (?), stamped, resealed, and sent on. How many working hours were wasted on her letters alone? Counting holidays as writing days, there could have been many more.

I can imagine my father sometimes sighing in despair, "Another letter from *Die Alte*, and she always wants something."

In her first letter, she wanted my father to search for the missing Georg Sacher, which seems rather crass, selfish and insensitive. And in many of her subsequent letters, she kept asking my father to find the unwanted stepfather. Was she so desperate to find her husband and did not care about her son's feelings? I imagine my father just shook his head and did nothing.

My grandmother was unlucky enough to break the only petroleum lamp in Nikolai's house. His wife was furious because, for all those involved, this loss meant having to go to sleep even earlier, and for my grandmother it meant reduced reading and writing time. For my mother, it meant a trip to Salzburg over a mountain pass, a tedious search for the right size lamp, then packing and sending it, feeling it would never arrive anyway. But actually, after three months, the package arrived undamaged. The landlord paid the 48 *roubles* tax, as my grandmother, the unpaid servant and lodger had no money at all.

Over the course of his life my father recorded, collected, catalogued and created huge files of letters, bills, bank statements, dental visits, transcripts, invitations: everything that seemed important to him was filed away. He filled a whole cupboard. Of course, all my grandmother's letters were filed, in date order, in a folder labelled in large red letters *'Die Alte'*. The envelopes were mostly thrown away, with the date of receipt noted on the first page.

When my father died, my brother showed no interest in this inheritance. Therefore, this dusty folder, which contains all my grandmother's letters from Russia, came to me. It was only when I started to write about her life that I began to study these letters; thank God they were easy to read and not written in the old-fashioned *Kurrent* (gothic) script. At my first glance through the letters, I was very surprised at the amount of gossip and the interest my grandmother found in it. Did the gossip simply remind her of the good old days and help her to retreat from her current unpleasant situation?

All the letters were worded for the censors, saying that she was well and she had enough to eat and was longing for a family reunion. She cursed the *Führer* in English and wrote 'such an idiot' – but there was never a bad word about any Russian leader, about her situation or about the Russians.

Her handwriting radiated strength, no wobbly lines, no misspelling, no corrections. At this point I must mention that my mother was a graphologist by profession. She scrutinised every letter, dissected her mental state, and looked for clues into her psyche. She found no ambiguity in her thoughts; all were clearly formulated, as were the desires, the questions and the offensive swipes at various family members. Her unwavering letter strokes radiated strength and hope even in the most adverse circumstances. "*Die Alte* will survive it all with her vitality and will to live."

Dutifully, my father and sometimes my mother replied to all the letters. But my parents never talked about these letters to us children; they were a source neither of joy nor of expectation. I have the suspicion that my father simply wanted to forget his mother, whom he had once loved so much. He did not need her in his life now, but she needed him since he was the only link to her missing husband and to freedom.

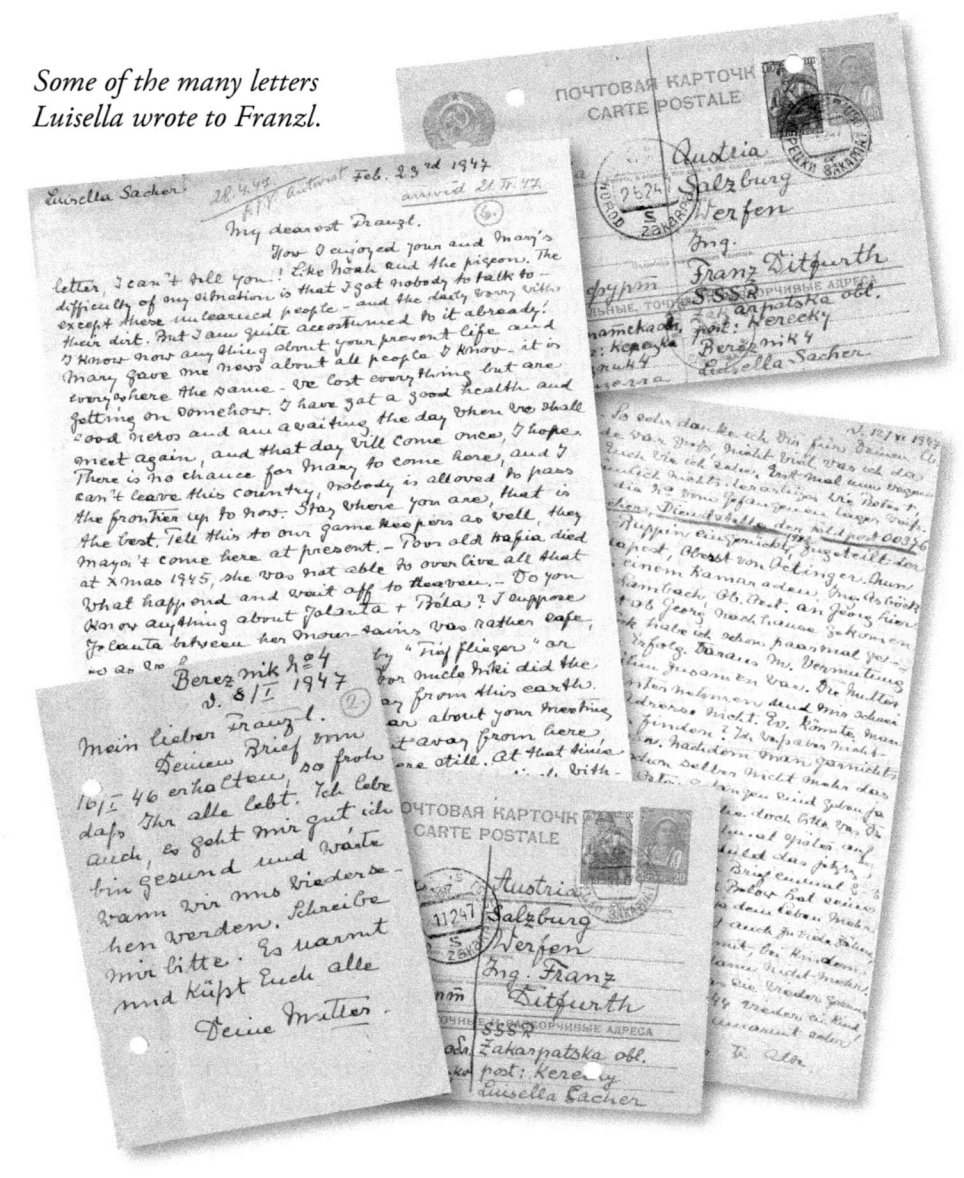

Some of the many letters Luisella wrote to Franzl.

Diogenes in the barrel

*A quarter of an hour of spring
is worth more than a sack of gold*

❀

While *Die Alte* was reporting on her life in Russia, which became less promising day by day, she saw herself as Diogenes living in the barrel, a famous myth from Greek mythology. She mourned the loss of her stolen Waterman pen, which forced her to borrow the schoolgirl's leaky pen. A double page torn from the exercise book gave her four pages to write on.

It was 4th August 1947:

"My dear Franzl.
We are once again living through a period of intermission; the post is having a rest! Not much new has happened here. People harvest all the hay as late as ever here. They wait until the hay is hard and withered – you know how conservative they are – the same as 200 years ago. They don't learn new things. But we have to let them know that in today's times this also has its advantages: they produce everything themselves, weaving, spinning and making their shoes, postale, out of the inner tubes of old tires. I now have inner-tube shoes too, light as a feather and comfortable, but as they are made of rubber, they're hot, so the feet cannot breathe properly and perspire. Then, by way of domestic industry, they are now producing cooking pots made of aluminium from crashed aircraft, if they can get their hands on the material. The pots are very useful. All business is done by bartering: for example, chicken for corn, potatoes for postale, sugar for beans, and pots for hay. My job now consists of looking after the houses while the families of the neighbourhood go into the fields for the day and I have to supervise their possessions and feed the

pigs, make lunch and whatever else there is to do. But the most difficult task is to keep an eye on the apple and plum trees since the countless local children are always trying to plunder them. These cheeky boys are a chapter in themselves. Under the new [communist] *regime a new law was introduced this year saying that the farmers have to give away milk, grain and hay, according to the size of their plot, which they don't like. The trains run infrequently since the Slovaks returned to their homeland. I envy the people who can leave; if only Austrians could leave too and I could come to you. Please inquire, as I have already asked you, whether the Austrian or the Russian representation in Vienna could do something; as I'm only an old woman, I'm quite uninteresting. We have had peace for more than two years now and nothing is happening. I have not yet been to Munkács but I am thinking that I can get away from here in 1-2 weeks, when we have finished haymaking, and then I will look for winter quarters. It is also easier to find out what is happening in a city; here one is so completely isolated and the people are only full of gossip, never anything intelligent. When they see a plane, they still believe there will be bombs; that's their mentality. This year's harvest was quite good, though hay is sparse; May was hot and dry. In our house* [she means Čonak] *and also in the administration building, 60 Russian children at a time are housed for a period of recreation, different ones every month. In Beregvar* [our friends, the Schönborns' estate] *adults are accommodated in the same way. In Beregvar, however, everything is intact, even the greenhouse is functioning, and the roses are thriving as usual. My longing for all you loved ones is intense, what wouldn't I give for a chat with you? And to see the children. I am so tanned that any Viennese summer holidaymaker would be filled with envy at my brown legs; stockings do not exist and going barefoot is the fashion. Unfortunately, it is August already and the summer is coming to an end – sad, because the winter is a tough time. Greetings from me to everyone I know, and hugs to all four of you.*

To you a big kiss from your,

Die Alte"

My grandmother never used paragraphs when she wrote because every centimetre of paper had to be used. This was her most revealing letter about the conditions in the country, with the least gossip about acquaintances, whom I knew only vaguely by name. Nor did she ask my father this time to find her husband. Even during those harsh years, her sense of humour never failed her, and the sharpness of her tongue was forever present, which another letter, this time to my mother, highlighted:

> "*What you wrote about the children was very interesting and I was only sad about Balthi's* [my brother's] *many teeth – this too is inherited from Franzl. I could do nothing as he was still small, and as the Ditfurth family was against all this kind of thing* [such as pulling teeth], *which could easily have fixed the problem. But they swallowed homeopathic pills wholesale to treat everything. Living in this family was like living in a house full of fools. Do not expect too much of Chrissi's* [that's me] *beauty – beautiful children are rarely beautiful adults; I'm warning you in confidence, don't be disappointed later on. Max Osterrieth* [her cousin] *was such a beautiful child that people stopped in the street to look at him – and later it was all lost. Rejoice in it, but everything is transient. Franzl was a very pretty child too. The main thing is that they grow up to become good and decent people – educate them in the spirit of English fair play, which is so important; all the hypocrisy around us is so disgusting. And I think that the world of the future will be in a way free from all falsehoods and dishonesty. All this Hitler-stuff is a joke, it was all lies and deceit, I could not stand it.*"

Actually, it was very unkind and tactless to have written such a letter. At that point my father could easily have said to himself, "*Die Alte* is so mean, always bitching about the family, never a kind word, why should I bother anymore?" He underlined the cutting passages with a red pencil and filed this letter with the previous ones. My father was very good looking, a handsome man all his life, who turned the heads of women in the street, and I never ceased to be proud of having such a good-looking father. Instead of rejoicing and congratulating my parents on their beautiful daughter, she could only criticise and be nasty. Did this letter hurt my parents or did they simply say: "*Die Alte* has not changed and never will"? It could have been envy, because she herself was never described as a beautiful child.

Anyway, my father was obviously worried as to whether his mother had enough clothes. Her answer to that was:

> "*By the way, do not worry about my outer appearance; it's lovely of you to want to dress me, but what little I have on me I am not ashamed of –*

'poor but clean'. I am beyond all ambition for myself, but would enjoy all the achievements of culture, for example an outhouse – we have none here and it is pretty much the same everywhere."

By this she meant that there was no lavatory in most of the houses, as was the case at Nikolai's house, and so she got used to doing her 'business' in nature just as she would have done while on hunting excursions. At -20° Celcius and in a snowstorm, I imagine this would be very uncomfortable. To wash, she went almost three kilometres to the nearest stream, the Poljanski, which she knew well from her fishing days and catching crayfish.

"I never looked 'poor', and that is the main thing, the certain something that one brings into the world; if one is not born on the dung heap, one can survive even wearing postale. I've become so accustomed to the latter that I often wear them; they are definitely warm and comfortable."

The first two winters she had to survive without a coat, in freezing cold weather with wind blowing right into her bones. For me that would be unimaginably hard to cope with. But still, she did not despair:

"When you're walking, you don't need much on; only if you are travelling is it bitterly cold as one travels here in open cattle trucks. But the country is not big, the trips are never long. Sometimes you travel in open utility trucks."

Suddenly the official stamp was missing on her letters, which made me think, that from now they were no longer censured. In her Christmas letter of 1947, she wrote that she had acquired a heavy woollen winter coat from a fallen soldier:

"The poor man is dead but for me his coat is a godsend and a wonderful luxury. It is so warm and practical."

Time ticked by slowly, and she never found new winter quarters in Munkács. After her three-year existence as a maid, she was finally able (with the help of my parents) to obtain an Austrian passport and a homeland pass through the authorities in Moscow; this brought her a big step closer to coming home. Her morale rose accordingly:

"Now the most important issue is to get a visa from the police station in Uzhgorod. If I get that, and since I am an old woman, there should be no

further hold ups, which would mean that I can come to you. And every day there is a direct train from Chop via Budapest to Vienna. How long it takes I do not know but I would use this train, so help me God. In this case, I wouldn't need to stay in Budapest, but would go straight through to Vienna. Once I am in Vienna it is all easy, if I do not go crazy with joy! Strange, just a year ago, I got the first message from you on 20th December, 1946 and finally knew that all of you are alive and today, exactly a year later, there is the prospect that I can come to you!"

Well, she could have come a lot earlier had she accepted the offer of her Jewish friends.

Indeed, she decided to stay and was now struggling with the authorities of the newly formed Soviet Union for her departure, not knowing what else was to come.

Munkács Castle.

Captured and frustrated

Knowledge colours a person more than paint

❋

Six months later she wrote again:

"My dear Franzl.

I only briefly answered your last letter of 2nd December 1947 with a postcard, since in the last two weeks I have been very busy organising my papers for my possible departure. This terrible weather – we almost drowned twice here, it rained uninterruptedly for three weeks, everything that had been saved up in the summer came down on us. Presumably it was similar where you are. Now it has not rained for two days and one can breathe, but it is as warm as in March [it was 25th January], *God has gone crazy! I submitted my passport and my papers on the 21st; when there will be a decision is written in the stars. But I am in good spirits and hope for the best. I am an eternal optimist and already see myself in my mind at the Ostbahnhof in Vienna, if it still exists."*

Then came the usual gossip about relatives and friends, this time underlined in red by my father. She continued:

"I have stopped myself from feeling sorry for the dead because they have stopped living. Life has not been a joyride, which in my opinion it never was. Nevertheless, something can be made out of everything. That I will never see the 'Pole meadow' [where she mostly worked] *again is not 100 per cent certain, it could still happen. I'm not laughing at you – everyone lives in their façon* [she loved to use French words now and again] *because nobody can avoid their fate. One should not even try and so I followed my path too in the hope it may soon lead me to the Ostbahnhof in Vienna!"*

After this followed a lot of family gossip. And then:

"I am very grateful to Maria for her efforts in Vienna on behalf of my departure. Let us hope that it goes well, but you can never know. In any case don't send anything here directly, only via the Foreign Office, because I don't seem to get anything that is sent directly."

More gossip, this time about her brother, whom she always found fault with. She continued:

"I embrace all four with all my heart and with kisses! Please keep your fingers crossed for me!
Always your faithful,
Die Alte.
PS: Did you get his birth data? Georg Wilhelm Sacher, born in Neuwelt – Harrachsdorf, 7 April 1913. Novy Svet – Harrachov (Sudeten).
Very grateful if you could continue to search! I write Russian quite well already; if only I had better paper and pens."

Did my father make any effort to find his unwanted stepfather, his junior by two years? I doubt it. Her next letter to my father in Austria was returned to her as undeliverable. Now she got worried: had we been scooped up by the Communists who were keen to deport all remaining foreigners. After all we were still Hungarians. What went wrong? Was it the mood of the post office? Hoping, my grandmother just re-sent the letter which eventually did arrive in Tenneck.

Here is what she had to say – 30th November, 1947:

"On December 8 I will think of you a great deal; 36 years old, my dearest! Getting closer to 40! The best years were at the Theresianum; I think of those untroubled times so often. I now have quite a lot of work knitting, which I get paid for, because 'Diogenes in the barrel' also needs a few pennies sometimes. You as a farmer will understand how I am often amazed at the ignorance of the local people with regard to livestock – what decent livestock they could have if they cared a little more and used common sense! But one cow after another becomes sick and has to be slaughtered because of filthy stabling, with sheep and goats getting smaller and more ragged as a result of inbreeding, and because they do not value

the males. In the past, the government authorities sometimes brought in good breeding sheep or goats; now they are left to their own devices, and there is hardly a single good sheep or goat – they're all lame, just like the cattle. But they cannot be told anything and they work in their own way, now no one is teaching them at all. They should all be 'damned', that's all I can say."

Ever hopeful, she awaited her departure and wrote in a letter a few weeks later:

"My dear Franzl.

Unfortunately, I cannot tell you anything new – I am waiting for my passport, and now five weeks have gone by, but you have to continue to hope, and slowly it's becoming warmer and the days are already considerably longer, which I, relying on scarce petroleum, find very pleasant. Must go again to my dental technician this week; my teeth are in great need of repair! Thank God, he is a Jewish dentist who is very well disposed towards me."

I wonder if she had hidden him in the forest during the German occupation.

"Unfortunately, Pepi has no talent for writing addresses in Cyrillic on envelopes – no letter has come from her. I do not know what she is doing, but she is incapable of writing the correct address. It's like the Jews, no letters have come from them either, their Schreibsel [scribble], is equally hair-raising. I've seen the most ridiculous things, but they cannot be taught. They mix everything together, Russian, Latin and Yiddish, which ends up completely unintelligible. The uneducated Jews, like ours here, lost their equilibrium during deportation when they were not allowed to practice their religion. The cultured Jews in Munkács have, of course, remained the same. Their education is the one thing that survives everything, whereas a deficiency in education, or a complete lack of it, makes people quite unstable. I have had the time and opportunity to study people in all situations and can only say that a pedigree English dog is far more agreeable than a local stray. I still grieve for my Angora cat [His Lordship]; what a gentleman he was. If only I could have another such animal, but in my present circumstances that is impossible.

If ever I get away from here, it will be a pleasure not to have to contend with the Rusnak's incompetence at farming and breeding, which always turns my stomach. They do not want to learn anything; they could have observed many things over the years. I bought some fabric for a dress, which I want to make myself for Easter. Previously such material would only have been good for a lining. I have 'a good soul' in Svalava who cuts the pattern; sewing machines are available here in the village. I'll finish now so that I can send this letter off tomorrow and it is getting dark.
A big hug with kisses and a thousand good wishes for the three birthdays in April." [my brother, me and our mother]
Die Alte"

She wrote the above letter on 27th March, 1948 – already three years after the end of the War.

It never occurred to her that during all these months of waiting, the authorities would gather evidence against her. Čonak was a well-run estate in which justice and order prevailed; three generations of owners were socially minded and always looked after people's welfare. As a 'doctor' and nurse, my grandmother saved many lives. However, her stern sense of order did breed enemies, and in the new social order, as a landowner, she had turned into an enemy of the Soviet State.

In the next letter of 11th April, 1948, she announced that she had received two parcels of land. When I read that, the thought shot through my head, wondering if she ever visited the grave of her first husband, my grandfather, who lay directly behind the fields she had described. Unfortunately, I neglected to ask, but since she never mentioned the grave in any of her letters, I suppose she did not find time for it.

As always, she gossips about different friends from the past and slightly varied the way she signed.

My grandmother's letters mostly included a request, first to seek her missing husband, then came the broken petroleum lamp, and after that a constant plea for her departure from behind the Iron Curtain. The strain on my parents was constant, especially since they lived in Tenneck, a small place with no access to any government department. They faced their own problems: my father collapsed in 1945, the year in which the War finally ended. He contracted infectious jaundice, which he could not shake off. As a result, his diaphragm ceased to function and a number of X-rays were unable to diagnose the problem. He could barely breathe and only with great difficulty managed one flight of stairs from his office up to our apartment. In Tenneck, with only a village doctor, without money or further assistance, it was a suggestion of the local doctor to take him to the psychiatric clinic in nearby Schwarzach St. Veit. No one knew how to help. My loving mother kept this great concern away from us children. It is thanks to her that my father recovered after three years because she identified the problem, massaged his diaphragm and eventually cured him. His illness was never mentioned in any letters, it was our private problem. Could bad news from us have taken the wind out of *Die Alte*'s sails? Even though our lives had also changed for the worse, we still had beds, warm rooms and a bathroom – a life of luxury indeed.

> "My dear Franzl.
>
> *It is Pentecost once again and I have time to write now because in the coming weeks we have to start chopping wood and then I'll be too tired in the evening. I'll be glad when the chopping season comes to an end, as my back is getting old and I'm feeling it; luckily my Schönberg legs are holding up well. There are millions of flies here in the country now; it is a blessing that they at least leave you in peace during the night. Here in Bereznik seven houses burned down a week ago – poor people, the wooden houses burned like tinder and they managed to save almost nothing. I do not know if I wrote to you that I go to the Baptist Church and usually spend Sundays there; it is very similar to our religion. I find all the singing in the Orthodox Church, unless it is done with splendid Byzantine pomp, very monotonous and boring. It is interesting how Baptist churchgoers – there are only a few of them – are sticking together, maintaining their rituals and always in good spirits. Moses's Ten Commandments are sufficient to keep everything in order. The people have a lot of imagination, it's in their nature, and the Baptists have positive values about themselves – whilst the others believe that the world is full of horror stories. One only gets to believe what one sees with one's own eyes, everything else is wrong. No mail has arrived since the two letters in May. As to my application, of course, nothing has changed – I go on waiting."*

By now it was the middle of June, 1948. My grandmother celebrated her 60th birthday as a farmer's maid. In Germany, the Marshall Plan came into effect. On 21st June, the Deutschmark was born and with it, foreign trade. This was the beginning of the economic boom – the *Wirtschaftswunder*. Her situation did not change and she celebrated Christmas in 1948 again with Nikolai and his family.

In another letter, written on 9th February, 1949, we were given an insight into their family life:

> *"The farmer's wife, Madame Nikolai, is in a prolonged horrible mood, and life with her is no pleasure at all. Uneducated people like her lack the most basic self-control, and animals and humans in Madame's vicinity have to suffer because of it – even though they are entirely innocent. One evening her eldest daughter, who has been married for three years, was caught by her husband in flagrante with a young lover, whereupon he threw her out. Nikolai saw the matter in a philosophical way, and simply said, "She is not coming back into my house". But mother indignantly argues with her husband and son-in-law and claims everything is a lie and her daughter is innocent! I must say, as a neutral observer, that the daughter has already had three adorateurs* [lovers] *in her short marriage, so the mother is quite wrong, and the daughter's husband and her father are perfectly right to throw her out. But nonetheless, we two, the little girl and I, must pay for Madame's foul mood."*

I often wondered what was worse for my grandmother: the mental frustration during her four years of peasant life or being physically stuck in the Soviet Union? As an educated woman, who could discuss any topic in German, French, English, Dutch and Russian, it would have been demeaning for her to talk only about subjects such as chickens, pigs, dogs, food and other mundane things. No world news, no radio, no telephone. Reading and writing were the only intellectual stimuli she had.

Again, and again she wrote:

> *"The people are so terribly uneducated and primitive. If only I could talk to somebody educated. I have organised for myself some good reading matter: a German Bible borrowed from the carpenter. The Old Testament has always interested me: firstly, I am an admirer of Moses, and secondly, everything is so human with the old prophets. Also, how*

life now in many respects reminds us of the Greek gods, who also have so much wisdom about life. I also have a good relationship with the Rabbi, and I'm always borrowing books from him."

At the end of every summer, she remarked that she wanted to find winter quarters in Munkács. But then it never worked out. I have a strong suspicion that no one wanted her, for two good reasons: first, she was the Baronesa, a capitalist, and nobody wanted to expose themselves to the Communist regime by sheltering a capitalist, and secondly, anyone who knew grandmother's character also knew that despite her good qualities, she would not be easy to live with. She remained banished in the pigsty.

On the 9th February, 1949, she wrote a letter to my mother. Most of the four pages were taken up with the weather, her visa requests, her living conditions – gossip about family and friends moved into the background. By now *Die Alte* had already celebrated four Christmases in the kitchen-cum-dining-room-cum-bedroom with Nikolai and family. She hadn't given up hope yet, but her patience was coming to an end.

In the same year in Austria, Mr Gmeiner founded the SOS *Kinderdorf*, a charity for children who were orphaned during the War. His idea was to accommodate a group of children in one house with a housemother caring for them, thus replicating a family home. It turned out to be a huge success and the concept has since been copied all over the world. My grandmother would have highly approved. She wrote a letter to my mother.

"*My dear Maria.*

For a long time, I have not heard from you; the last letter was at the end of November – since then there has been nothing. Here once again they are busy with my travel documents. They interviewed people who knew me, etc. and passed all the information over to bureaucrats in Svalava; so now they have been dealing with my papers for over two months, but there is nothing tangible, no definite hope to be seen. It's no good; I'll just have to wait until it is my turn. I am writing it down just so that you know that they are dealing with me. I would be so glad if I could leave in the spring and not have to tend this miserable bit of field where nothing will ever grow again without some manure. As an old farmer and gardener, this mismanagement is particularly annoying for me. The winter with its snow and cold weather continues. It has been a long cold winter; at the end of November the frosts started and since then it has been constantly cold and miserable. I was hoping that it would ease off in February but, on the contrary, it is still very cold. The children would have had lots of tobogganing. Has Franzl taught his son to ice skate yet? So he can follow in his father's footsteps and become an ice hockey star? Then, like me, he can spend the evenings at the ice rink enthusiastically admiring his son."

It seemed that in her imagination we still lived in Vienna, in her familiar surroundings. The fact that Tenneck did not offer the opportunity to ice skate and that we could only dream of the elegant Viennese ice skating club did not cross her mind; past and present seemed blurred. We did have ice skates: that is, we strapped irons to our leather ski boots. My father had rescued his old hockey shoes and impressed us enormously when he showed us his tricks on the frozen pond beside the railway. The uneven natural ice made its demands on us, but I could soon skate backwards and even do a jump. I dreamed of becoming an ice princess. My brother showed little ambition on the ice, but later his son, my nephew, became an enthusiastic ice hockey player.

Grandmother's letters to my mother always contained more gossip about old friends and family than her letters to my father. On 16th April, 1949, she dreamed of her arrival in Vienna:

"I will somehow get by and stay with some of my friends; some of them are still alive and will help me. I am not helpless, and in the last three and a half years of my life nothing has damaged me – I have taken to my current life just like a duck to water. The only question is how I will find my place in civilisation again. But I think that will come quickly, because everything does if one has no choice. My inquisitive mind is still quite the old one, mixed with Russian equanimity, because that's necessary here – so that nothing can faze you. Nothing would bother me if only I were in Vienna already! But heaven only knows when this will be; for the time being, nothing is happening. In March they asked me three times to go to Svalava to the militia, always asking questions about my role in Čonak. They were apparently satisfied. As I mentioned before, a new official from Russia has had everything in his hands since the 1st March 1948 and is taking care of my case. I think that it would be good, and the Munkács Jews agree with me. To do something from Vienna – trying from both

ends; this would be the best. Only please refer to me as the widow Moriz Ditfurth, not Sacher, and write via Moscow, by letter. Sending anything directly to me is futile because it does not get into my hands."

Then, again, gossip and a lot of backbiting against the relatives, together with the familiar question:

"Tell me, hasn't anything come from the Red Cross [another reference to the missing husband]? *There should be an answer somewhere. It would be known by now if he had been killed in Budapest or taken prisoner of war. If he were free somewhere, he would have written to his mother. Write and tell me what prospects there are and be an angel and go to Vienna again with regards to my departure* [repatriation]. *Maybe it will help? The mail is so slow, and a letter from Moscow takes two weeks. Much, much love to you all, kisses to the children from the Russian baba, though of course they won't have a clue about me.*

Hugs & kisses to Franzl from your faithful,

Die Alte"

This next letter, which arrived after another letter written in April to my mother, appeared to have suddenly been censured. It was written on 4th March, 1949, with the usual beginning:

"My dear Franzl.

Earlier, I returned from a trip to Uzhgorod where I had been called because of my visa. After waiting three months for my request for departure to Austria to be granted, I still have some hope that I might be able to leave here in the foreseeable future. My trip to Uzhgorod was very cold and tedious. It does not want to get warm this year; it is now March and it is still just like January! An icy wind was blowing and waiting for the various means of transport in the open air, because there are no shelters, was no pleasure."

In this letter she allowed herself to get carried away complaining about her situation, ending the letter with:

"The winter has been abnormally cold; once again I froze to my bones, but my health is thankfully very good – except my nose, which runs all the time." (I inherited this runny nose from her.)

At the time of reading this letter from *Die Alte*, my father could not have known that this would be her last.

As always, he replied dutifully. But in months to follow his letter and subsequent ones came back with the stamp *'Retour – Parti'*.

What had happened? She had simply vanished. Shot dead, run over by a lorry, injured, taken prisoner?

I grew up thinking my grandmother was dead.

Revenge is sweet

*You can crush a man
with the weight of your tongue*

"If a Rusnak can read and write, he has made it in life," my grandmother said. During the hundreds of years of Hungarian administration of the Carpathians, no compulsory schooling existed. It was only after World War I, when the Czechs were awarded the Carpathians, that compulsory education was introduced. At the end of World War II, half the population was still illiterate. By now some clever young locals had worked out how to deal with newly arrived Russians and how to exploit the political situation to their advantage. The occupying Russian military needed the cooperation of the locals, the clever ones, who knew how to steal and cheat, to become part of the newly formed intelligentsia. They soon felt at home in the mayor's townhouse in Kerecky and the new courtroom of Uzhhorod (now Uzhgorod), the seat of a new form of justice. The 'rule of law' was emphasised with a grand ostentatious building with its high ceiling and pseudo-Greek columns. This pomp offered a perfect setting for showcasing power and intimidating anybody who rightly or wrongly came into contact with the law.

When the wealthy Hungarian landowners settled in the Carpathian Mountains hundreds of years ago, two opposite worlds with different values inevitably collided. The concept of private ownership – 'entry prohibited' – was totally foreign. The native population was accustomed to taking everything that could be taken. Poaching was a tradition, stealing anything (like timber) a sport, catching fish in the stream a question of dexterity, shooting game a question of having a gun. That forests and meadows were not to be exploited randomly by everybody was entirely alien to the locals. Right or wrong, yours or mine were concepts to be ignored. For the small farmers, it was easier to defend and protect their orchard and their fields against thieves than for the large landowners. It was one of the tasks of the Čonak gamekeepers to scare away poachers, who would shoot anything that roamed freely in the forest, regardless of the animal's welfare nor of the ownership of the Schönberg family. The poachers presented a daily challenge for the gamekeepers, who were familiar with the land and the game stock. They had a fair idea who the perpetrators were, delighting in playing 'cat and mouse', trespassing and shooting whatever came their way. There was one particularly crafty poacher who was young, determined, cunning and fast, always escaping the gamekeepers at the very last minute. He was a constant worry, and when Hermann, the chief gamekeeper, finally spotted him from behind a tree, he reached for his shotgun and shot him in the back. He proudly reported to my grandmother, "Baroness, I finally got him, and the pellets in his back will be a reminder for life."

And so they were!

As things turned out, the 'poacher' soon adapted to the new rules, was eager to show off his local knowledge and in no time worked his way up the bureaucracy through cunning and sycophancy. The 'poacher' knew everything about the Čonak estate which was helpful for the new owners, the Soviet State. This gave him additional power. And when the application for repatriation from the Baroness landed on his desk, he slapped his thigh, grinned with satisfaction, and pushed her request into the bottom drawer of his paper-laden desk.

World War II had been over for almost five years, and my grandmother was still awaiting her departure, unaware of where her application had ended up. For some time, the authorities had repeatedly requested information and documents and had interrogated her, without giving her a clue why. Nevertheless, she remained optimistic about getting permission to leave because, as so often in her life, she could not grasp reality. She believed she was only a useless old woman. From her point of view, the reason for the endless delays was the cumbersome bureaucracy, combined with proverbial Russian sloppiness. This meant that she was utterly surprised when she was summoned to the Uzhgorod courtroom, instead of the district office in Munkács, to undergo an official interrogation. A mock trial was held there and then.

With some suspicion, she entered the courtroom and recognised, to her great horror, the 'poacher' of Čonak, now a little older and rounder, well dressed with polished shoes and combed hair, sitting in the witness box. With a malicious grin on his face, he listened to the judge, who solemnly read out a long list of accusations about her mismanagement and maltreatment of employees in Čonak. You could blame her for a lot of things, but she never mistreated anybody. After all she was their 'doctor', 'midwife' and 'cash donor'.

As the judge read out the long list of accusations, the poacher, now the star witness, nodded approvingly. When the judge finally finished, declaring "Ten years Labour Camp in the Ural Mountains", the poacher triumphantly stood up and turned to my grandmother: "And you old *stari baba* (woman), you will not be going to the West but to the East – and enjoy it, should you survive it." She shot him a deadly look back and hissed in Russian, "And I shall survive it," turned around and stormed out of the courtroom with her head held high, now flanked by two Russian soldiers.

She never returned to the family, the little girl and the pigsty. The little girl of the Nikolai family lost her 'ally'. Nobody could work out what had

A map highlighting the main cities of Luisella's journey in Europe.

happened. The letters written by my parents were returned as undeliverable, rumours swirled around Bereznik. For everybody, each answer produced another question.

After a year had passed, my father put a cross by her name, which indicated that she was a deceased person.

From 1949 to 1955 my grandmother was a political prisoner. Her official crime was that she had violated paragraph 2a: she wanted to leave the Soviet Union, which was an offence against the State. For this criminal act, she was sentenced to 10 years in a Labour Camp. Now she belonged to the 1,230 statistically recorded and condemned Austrians who vanished within the Soviet Union between 1945 and 1955.

In Russia, a woman over 60 was classified as an invalid, which was a blessing for my grandmother, because she was officially too old to be forced to work, which made her imprisonment even more absurd. The Soviet Union now had to feed and clothe a useless 61-year-old invalid. As such, she was allowed to move around more freely, because at her age there was less danger of escape – although in fact my grandmother could have escaped faster than many people half her age. The real question was: where to? To absolutely nowhere.

After her arrest, her personal belongings, of which she had not many, were taken away. She was dressed as a Russian prisoner: black dress, black headscarf, thick quilted jacket, woollen stockings, and a pair of shoes that never fitted her properly – if I could only have my *postale*, she kept thinking. Since her own wardrobe had become so worn out, she found the prison clothes like haute couture.

But what bothered her most, and she protested vehemently in very strong language, was that her simple gold wedding ring was pulled off her finger. "I cursed and argued with the Russian official for a long time until he promised me that I would get the ring back upon my release: 'I guarantee you' (prisoners were seen as inferior and therefore addressed with the informal *du*)." Under the sharp gaze of my grandmother's eye, he attached the gold ring by a thread to the first page of her documents, pushed her file into a brown envelope, which he sealed with a lick and pushed it into a drawer. Then he handed her the confirmation slip with the triumphant smile of an *apparatchik*. Still angry, she took the piece of paper and never parted with it. This ring was the last connection with her beloved young husband. Had the wedding ring, for my otherwise unromantic grandmother, become a symbol of their love pact? I wonder if her husband still had his ring on his finger?

After completion of the paperwork, she was taken without delay to the railway station in Uzhgorod and thrown into a waiting railway carriage, which was collecting prisoners for deportation.

As with all prisoners, this was the worst episode of her life. Humans were degraded to mere animals. For example, you were only allowed to go to the toilet twice a day, for half a minute in the morning and again in the evening; if you had to go at any other time, you were beaten, kicked and robbed of your clothes, and whatever food you had was stolen. And of course, Russian soldiers repeatedly pestered you. As a result of this completely unrealistic rule, most of the prisoners had no choice but to wet themselves. In a compartment made for 10 people, 20 or more were crammed in, and if the journey was in a cattle train, up to 60 people would be stuffed into a single wagon. This was especially bad for my grandmother, who was small in stature, because the smell of urine rose directly into her nose as she was wedged between strangers. It was a huge advantage to be tall, she would later recount.

She also complained about the frequent stops for controls, which could take place at any time of day or night and were an additional torture, because you either had to find some space in the narrow corridor to make yourself visible or had to get off the train for inspection. Because a prisoner in transit was not working, so to speak, he or she did not deserve any food. Sometimes there was one herring and one loaf of bread to last three days.

For my grandmother, the first journey was only 243 kilometres, because she went from Uzhgorod directly to a prison in Lemberg, today's L'viv, where hell on earth was waiting for her. Serving as a transit prison, each cell was packed with prisoners and was so crowded that there was standing-room only. However, my grandmother, the invalid, was allowed to lie down on the damp stairs outside the cell during the night. She recounted:

"What shortened these nights – because sleeping on the cold, damp stairs was impossible anyway – was the cat that belonged to a prison guard. It was great fun to watch how cleverly the cat caught the rats that were running around me. The cat pounced, sank her teeth into the rats, then shook them violently and bashed them against the steps until they were dead. That was fun to watch. But after a little while, I found it better

and warmer to stay in the cell; as there was no room to lie down, I trained myself to sleep standing up and after a few nights I was able to sleep quite well. Only the terrible stench of urine and sweat in the cell was unpleasant."

But among the hundreds of female prisoners from all social backgrounds and all corners of Russia, there was one ray of sunshine for my grandmother: a fellow Austrian inmate called Dr Margarethe Ottillinger. "After all those years, talking to an educated person, speaking German again, was an enormous pleasure," she enthused with a big smile.

Dr Ottillinger and the Baroness

*Truth can only be understood by
understanding its opposites*

On 5th November, 1948, the most spectacular abduction in Austrian history happened when Russian soldiers stopped the car of Minister Krauland with Dr Margarethe Ottillinger at his side. This happened on the Ennsbrücke, which served as the demarcation line and checkpoint for the Russian zone of divided and occupied Austria. She was arrested on the spot and accused by the Russians of spying for the Americans. Indeed, the brilliant 29 year old Ottillinger moved frequently between enemy camps, charged with the task of turning war production industries into peacetime factories. The incident happened within seconds, yet quick as a flash she threw the briefcase full of top secret information into the lap of her boss before she was dragged out of the car and disappeared. Nobody knew where to. Her boss, the Minister, saved through his status of immunity just clutched the briefcase, continued the journey and made no effort to save her.

Sometime in the latter part of 1949, my grandmother met her in the women's camp in Lemberg, which served as a 'transit lounge'. What a fortunate coincidence for both ladies in a miserable situation.

The immensely qualified economist had had a brilliant career and was the first woman to hold such high office in the government of Austria. Whether her arrest was a betrayal by her own government or a tactical game by the Russians remains unclear to this day. Did she tell my grandmother her version of events?

While Ottillinger, who was 30 years younger than my grandmother, repeatedly tried to commit suicide, for example by hanging herself from a windowsill with her nylon stockings, my grandmother never considered such measures as a possible way out of her plight. Later in life she sometimes quipped, "I'm going to kill myself," but this throwaway remark was probably a plea for love, which she eternally craved.

Ottillinger found God during her imprisonment and remained deeply religious for the rest of her life. She would later be honoured as the founder of the modernist *Votruba Kirche* (Wotruba Church) in Vienna-Liesing, and the square in front of the church was named *Ottillingerplatz*. My grandmother remarked: "Some people have religion; some people need religion." With that, the topic was closed. Ottillinger needed religion and clearly did not have the same genetic survival skills and unflinching optimism as my grandmother. Her imprisonment was physically much more brutal than my grandmother's – she was used to provide 'horsepower'. Shockingly, the theory was that seven women replace one horse and she was one of seven. Although she resumed her remarkable career after returning to Austria, she never recovered from the Soviet Union experience. My grandmother, on the other hand, determined to survive everything, displaying no physical or mental deficiencies after her return.

In Lemberg during their months 'in hell', both women appreciated each other's company. During one of their chats, they realised that they had a common acquaintance in Vienna: Emil Weinberger, a close friend of my father's who had often been a hunting guest in Čonak. Many wonderful memories came back to life and took away the grim reality of the day.

After about two months, their paths parted. In different cattle-trains, they were sent deep into the heartland of Russia assigned to Gulags, where they both spent the next six years in captivity.

Two months after her return, on 28th July, 1955, Ottillinger wrote the following letter to Emil Weinberger, the then President of the Chamber of Commerce in Vienna:

"Dear Dr Weinberger,

Thank you very much for your kind welcome, which I was really looking forward to. I am already refreshed and energised, but still need to go to the mountains to recuperate my health.

I met an older woman in Lemberg prison who knows you very well, since you were friends with her son, and you have often been a guest in her house. If I remember rightly, this lady had an estate in the Huzulen country. She also told me that her son lived in Austria and was working for you in Tenneck. Unfortunately, I have forgotten her name. She was a very dear person and very brave, although she was already quite white-haired, and our life in Lemberg could only be compared to a nightmare.

I would be interested to know whether her description of you is correct; her narrative about you seemed accurate. She had been sentenced to 10 years.

I would like to thank you for your kind words and remain, with best greetings,

Margarethe Ottillinger"

The Austrian Press announced on 6th May, 1955, that Dr Ottillinger had been released from captivity. She was gravely ill and carried off the train on a stretcher. My grandmother jumped off the train three months later.

Both of them benefitted from Stalin's death in 1953, which loosened the reins in the Soviet Union.

On the 15th of May, 1955, the Austrian State Treaty was signed in Vienna. Austria became a free and independent sovereign state again.

At that time my grandmother was still a prisoner of war.

The two ladies never met again.

Franzl with Emil Weinberger as students, on a winter hunt in Čonak.

Life in the Gulag

*Never think – here no one can see me –
I can let myself go*

❋

Molotov, the then Foreign Minister and a protégé of Stalin's, declared on 8th March, 1931, "We have never concealed the fact that in certain projects we employ a labour force of healthy and work-fit prisoners. We did it then and are doing it now and we will continue to do it in the future. The exact number is a state secret." It is estimated that there were up to 500 camps in the Soviet Union which all benefitted from this huge supply of free labour. The biggest camp, Vortuka, had 73,000 prisoners! The Gulags held robbers, thieves and murderers, but also people who had committed minor offences, such as being late for work. For example, if someone was late three times, he was sentenced to three years in a Gulag. Jokes about political parties could cost somebody 25 years. If someone stole potatoes or barley from a field that had belonged to him before Stalin's Expropriation Act, it could mean up to 10 years' imprisonment.

My grandmother was one of the estimated 14 million prisoners between 1923 and 1953 in the Gulags (corrective labour camps) of the Soviet Union, which had originated in Poland, and were also called 'Administration for Fine Work'. In reality, it meant the exploitation of humans under the most inhumane conditions.

On the very first night after my grandmother's return, my mother could wait no longer to ask her a burning question: "I dreamt about you quite intensely about a year ago; you were barefoot in a black dress, sitting on a wooden stool; you seemed healthy and had snow-white hair, which was wonderfully styled. This dream was so vivid that from then on I was convinced you were alive."

With a toothless smile she explained, "Maria, your dream was totally real. In the men's camp was a Frenchman – a political prisoner – who was captured in Moscow when he was visiting his Russian wife's parents. She was an opera singer; he was the hairdresser at the Paris Opera. Since I often served as an interpreter in the men's camp, I met him soon after my arrival and on Saturdays, when we were allowed to visit the men's camp, I used to talk with him in French while he did my hair. We chatted animatedly about God and the world. As you dreamt, my hair has never been so well styled in my life as it was when I was a prisoner."

My well-read father was in the habit of writing comments in every book, always in pencil, and underlining what was of particular interest to him. On the first page of every book, he would note when and on what occasion he had received or bought the book. He also put relevant cuttings inside his books. Sometimes the books ended up badly distorted by the cuttings and fell apart. Among hundreds of books, I found a little black booklet entitled *Forced Labour in the Sowjet Union*, published in Vienna in 1953.

My father gave this booklet to *Die Alte* soon after her return, asking her to write her comments in it because he wanted to verify whether her experiences corresponded to what the book said. She duly added her remarks in pencil and underlined passages, which gave a clear account of what she had actually experienced.

In the chapter *'Prosecution and transport of persons who are condemned to compulsory labour'* my grandmother underlined the following passages[3]:

> *"On the way, terrible conditions prevailed, no matter what means of transport were used; they were the hardest thing the prisoners had to undergo during their punishment. The main means of transport was the railroad; it deserves to be mentioned first.*
>
> *The prisoners were picked up from the detention centre and, after a superficial medical examination and a review of their papers, were loaded into railway wagons. It is unbelievable how many people were packed into these freight trains with their meagre personal possessions. Once the train was loaded with its human cargo, the doors were closed. Often the trains did not leave immediately for their destination but remained standing in stations for days on end, exposed to wind and weather.*

Another string of atrocities had to be endured by political prisoners when they were placed amongst professional criminals [which was the case with my grandmother] *and had to watch these thieves robbing and harassing people. These hard-core criminals, the so-called 'Uriki', would surround the political prisoners in groups in order to take their food, clothing and other items. Or they stole any object they wanted before the eyes of their intimidated victims. If anybody complained to the guards, the complaint was ignored, because the guards would have opened themselves to acts of revenge by the Uriki. One of the criminals' favourite activities during their transport and later in the camps themselves was playing cards – gambling for items belonging to a member of the political class. Even before the game started, the Uriki would have picked an item of desire, which they then took off the hapless loser."*

There was nothing to steal from my grandmother's possessions other than her second pair of reading glasses, which she kept well hidden. Luckily, she had no gold fillings in her teeth: "The Uriki forced open the mouths of other prisoners in order to tear out the gold fillings; that was a terrible sight," she admitted.

The following paragraph of the book was vigorously underlined in pencil:

"Our carriage was attached to a scheduled train and overfull. If someone had to go to the toilet outside the appointed time, it was terrible. After repeated pleading, one was allowed to do so, but upon return one was beaten and kicked. Finally, the slow pace of the train taking people to the camps lengthened the misery for everybody. If the transport was heading for a camp in Northern Russia, the trip would take two to three weeks, but if Siberia was the destination, it could easily take one to two months.

For shorter destinations, the prisoners were sometimes loaded into open railway carriages without protection against rain and sun and left standing there for more than a week. Many of them fell ill and arrived at the camp in terrible shape, unable to work."

My grandmother was fortunate that her transport to the Urals took place towards the end of summer, sparing her any additional hardships.

After weeks of train travel, crammed in and half-starved, my grandmother's journey ended in the OLP/9 Camp Seljanka, near

Solikamsky, Molotovskaya Oblast, in the Ural Mountains, which represent the geographic boundary between Europe and Asia. The region is famous for its salt, magnesium and potassium-chloride mines.

A women's camp for 1,200 women, mostly Russians, awaited her there, as well as a men's camp for 1,000 men, who were gathered from far and wide. This Gulag was classified as small, since the sizes varied from 5,000 to 25,000 inmates. The criminal prisoners had an eagle tattooed on their backs and now, after the long train ride, were separated from the political prisoners in order to bring some peace and normality into camp life.

Everybody settled into the new routine which was well thought out: the women were used for fieldwork, while the men were put to work in the forests and mines. A high barbed wire fence with watchtowers surrounded the camp. Throughout the night, powerful searchlights beamed down on the wooden barracks so that no one could escape. It was probably more a waste of electricity than anything else. Where could anyone escape to in this remote region? Since the locals came begging to the camp, it was clear that the quality of life in the nearby villages was even worse. After initially

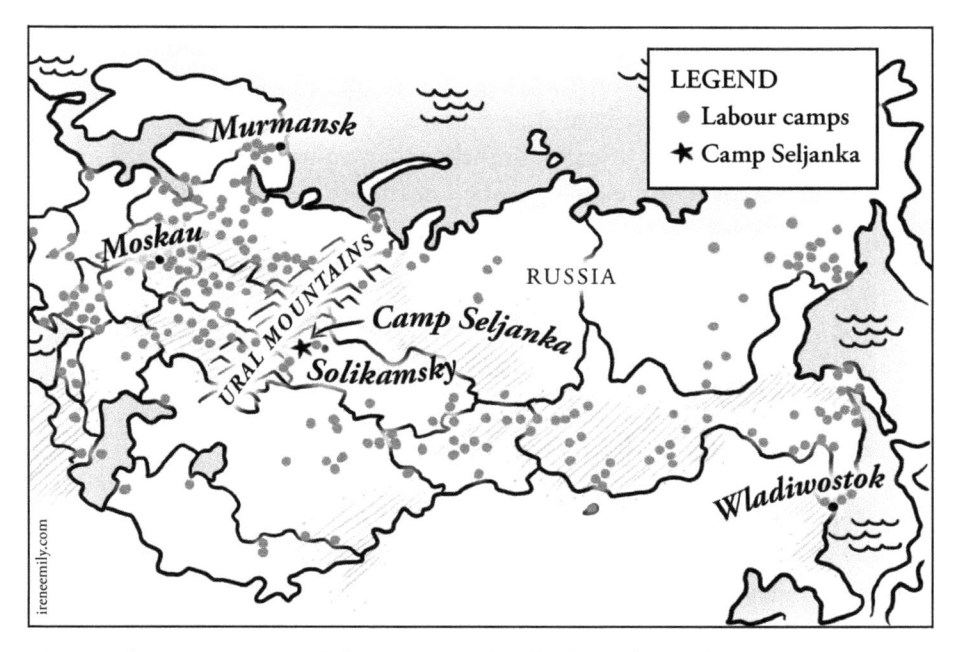

A map showing Russian labour camps (Gulags) in the early 1950s. Luisella was held at Camp Seljanka, near Solikamsky, from 1949 to 1955.

being housed with 20 or more women in one room, my grandmother was moved into a room with only five other women. "It was quite comfortable," she said. "Only when it was raining, we had to place buckets everywhere, because there were holes in the roof."

Some of her stories I remember well: "During the potato harvest our harvest was not measured by weight or quantity of potatoes, but only by a glance over the fields by the supervisor to check whether the green stems of any potato plants were still visible. The result was that half the crop rotted in the fields because it was much easier to simply stamp the stems of the plants, with their potatoes, into the ground rather than bending over and digging them out. With a glance across the fields, the supervisor found everything to be *karascho*, which is the Russian equivalent of OK."

There was minimal medical care. First Aid did not exist. Now and then an ambulance would come from Moscow. My grandmother said time and time again: "One had to stay healthy. The poor miners were the most vulnerable because they had to dig with their hands, without protective masks, in damp mining shafts, and mostly died of some kind of lung disease. The brutal reality was that dead men were simply replaced by a new batch of healthy ones. For us women, life in the camp was much easier, and my good fortune was that I never got sick. I just broke my little finger, which is still a bit bent, but that does not matter."

My then, 61-year-old 'invalid' grandmother, volunteered to work – what else would she have done all day. She became the 'sauna lady'. In winter, temperatures plummeted to between -20° and -40° Celsius, so a sauna was more a necessity than a luxury to warm up frozen bones and to dry wet clothes. My grandmother made sure that the temperature was correct, that hot water infusions were done properly, that the sauna was clean, that no one stayed too long and that no fights broke out. I have no idea if she herself enjoyed using the sauna. Since she was paid for her work, she had money to bribe with and to barter for cigarettes and liquor.

Very soon, with her authoritative character, fearless nature and sense of fair play, she was appointed, by the other women, Camp Brigadier. In this powerful position, she was responsible for the distribution of food. And food was always scarce and a reason to pick a fight. Justice came first, doing favours did not exist and helping herself was out of the question, even in the face of the most inviting temptation. "I was the only one who could always slice the bread exactly two centimetres thick. There was never a fist-fight among the hungry women during the distribution of food, since each of them knew they would get exactly the same portion. We never had fresh fruit or vegetables. We prisoners lived on soup, bread, potatoes and cabbage, the most valuable source of vitamins. Daily rations of cabbage and yet more cabbage made me hate cabbage. Please never give me cabbage again in my life." That was her first plea immediately after her return.

Twice a year there were inspection visits from Moscow. Because my grandmother was thought unlikely to escape, she was sent to the nearest town to do the shopping before such visits. In Solikamsky she had to buy red crepe paper at the only store in town for the purpose of *Maskirovka*, a well-loved word for 'disguise'. It was 'tradition' that all the dirt in the halls, the corridors, the kitchen and the canteen was swept under things or into various corners. The colourful crepe paper was then draped over the mess underneath and made everything look pretty for the inspection. A superficial glance pleased the eye and everything was *karascho* – just like the potato harvest.

My grandmother loved to tell this story because, in her eyes, it symbolised the futility of Communism.

Her shopping trips into the village extended to accompanying other women who had to go to a seamstress because everything they were wearing was falling apart, either torn or worn out, and had to be made wearable again. On these occasions, she had to buy liquor for the permanently drunk camp director. When he was drunk and molested the other women in the camp, she scolded him using the worst Russian swear words and booted him out of the room where he was pestering the intimidated women. That earned her enormous respect from her inmates and confirmed her status of Camp Brigadier. In the course of telling these stories, she would say, "*Nee*, you know, I was never scared and I was never beaten."

The alcoholic camp director had great respect for her and acknowledged her strength and hard work. Since he had three orphaned children who needed a woman to look after them, he asked her to marry him. She would then be able to have a Russian passport and live freely outside the camp. But had she done that, she would no longer be a 'missing person' and would never ever be able to leave Russia. When pressed for an answer to this generous offer, she delayed her reply, which was a definite no.

"The Russians could make alcohol out of everything! For example, old tea leaves were fermented and soaked in kerosene, which was then drunk as a house *Schnapps*. Consequently, the petroleum lamps were hardly used for their actual purpose, as there was always kerosene missing."

Just as we children learned the Salzburg dialect in Tenneck, my grandmother as a child in Čonak had learned Rusnakisch, the language of the local farmers. Now, in the camp, she improved her Russian language skills by learning to read and write the Cyrillic script. Every year she got better, which not only boosted her status amongst the mostly Russian women, but also helped her with her translation job in the men's camp.

She had always preferred men to women, and no man escaped my grandmother's discerning eyes. A young French footballer with a strong body and a fleshy 'potato' nose caught her attention. He had been a guest-worker in Poland when the Russians invaded and was simply arrested as a spy. Grandmother translated for him. She liked what she saw. "He became my protector." She smiled sheepishly at my mother with the explanation that she needed male protection against the many lesbians. She arranged for him not to be sent into the salt mines but to work in the forests, so that he would stay healthy and feel indebted to her. In no time, her life was organised to perfection: the French hairdresser for mind, soul and beauty, the young French footballer for personal safety and pleasure, and the drunken camp director wooing her for marriage.

When in 1955, two years after Stalin's death, the Seljanka women's camp was closed down, the alcoholic camp director pleaded with Luisella to stay, and delayed her release for months until she finally got on the last official homebound train, which arrived in Vienna on 25th July. Because of the continued need for workers in the mines and forests, the men's camp was not closed down. This meant that her friend and protector, who was still healthy and fit for work, could not leave. During their last embrace she whispered in his ear: "I will do everything for you to make it an *au revoir* in the West."

But before she could turn her back on Russia for good, there was still an important formality to be gone through: when she checked out at the release camp in Moscow, it was necessary to complete the final formalities for her discharge. The moment of truth had come when she could present the now completely crumpled receipt proving the ownership of her wedding ring. The clerk said *karascho*, took the paper and disappeared behind endless shelves full of files. *Die Alte* had already prepared a tirade of her best swear words, in order to let rip at Russian bureaucracy for one last time. She was looking forward to it and waited patiently. After 10 minutes or so, the clerk came back with a radiant smile on his face, waving her file. She opened it and found her wedding ring neatly attached to her documents, as if it was the most natural thing in the world. Since her arrest, six years had passed, and thousands of kilometres lay in between. Russian bureaucracy had functioned perfectly. She was speechless!

The intimate version

He who comes home is not the same as he who had left

❃

In the Gulag, during those monotonous days filled with hard work, Saturday was the most rewarding day for all the prisoners, not only because they were able to recover from work, but because the women were allowed to visit the men's camp.

This was a brilliant solution for all sexual tensions. My grandmother too looked forward to that day. The tone of her voice softened when she repeated the need for a protector against the lesbians. This explanation was accompanied by a coquettish smile flitting over her lips, which rang alarm bells in my mother's head. Not much more was said. However, my mother kept probing until she pieced together the puzzle of her intimate life in the Gulag. It took some weeks of detective work; she felt like Sherlock Holmes and sensed correctly that a lover was behind this familiar smile of her mother-in-law's.

On the very first evening after her return, the minute my father had gone to bed, my grandmother's voice became quieter, and in a business-like tone, she made a request: "Maria, there's this nice fellow still in the men's camp, a Frenchman, who was a guest-worker in Poland when the Russians invaded. I was his interpreter and he became my protector. He's a very decent fellow, who was sent to the camp totally innocently. Can you try to get him out with the help of our friend Hermann at the Ministry of the Interior in Vienna? You would be doing a really good deed. I am very anxious to help him."

Half of all the prisoners in the Gulags had never had a court ruling, conviction or final sentencing. They were simply labelled with an offence, for example as spies, because this was the quickest way to get free labour.

My mother, always helpful, replied, "I'll do my best."

Then a few days later, when my father had left the sitting room, my grandmother quickly changed the subject to the Frenchman again. By now my mother knew more – he was called Jean and he had been 32 years old when he arrived at the camp. "If you actually get him out, do you think you could find somewhere for him to work in the Lungau [she was contemplating settling there]? He was a very good football player and is a reliable worker. I urge you; can you please see what you can do!"

The Frenchman could not speak any German – that made finding a job in the country, where only a local dialect was spoken, much more difficult, with the unemployment rate in 1955 being 5.8 per cent. All of Europe was in the process of reconstruction. My mother asked around, but in vain – she was unable to find a job for Jean, her mother-in-law's protector and more than 30 years younger lover. However, there was still good news for *Die Alte*: after a few months, with the help of our friend and the Red Cross, it was actually possible to obtain Jean's release from the camp and get him out from behind the Iron Curtain.

Luisella got more and more excited. The date of Jean's return was imminent. She had long since decided she would meet him. She had exchanged the black prison dress for an elegant dark green silk dress, a present from my mother. She had started wearing pearls in her ears again and had a pearl necklace. By now she felt quite presentable. At her request, my mother booked a double room in a three-star hotel next to the train station in Strasbourg, Alsace. That request confirmed all suspicions. My grandmother wanted it to be known that she was still 'a catch' for a younger man. (I find myself thinking of the bedroom scene with Herr Sacher at the hotel in Budapest.) When she was driven to Werfen to catch the express train, my father and we children were told, "Your grandmother is just going to meet a newly released friend from the labour camp." My mother was very discreet and did not want to upset Franzl.

Three days later *Die Alte* returned from Strasbourg, alone. My mother was waiting for her at the train station in Werfen. This time she did not jump down the steps from the train, but appeared a broken woman, without a spring in her step. She briefly remarked, "*Ach*, Maria, Jean went on to his family in France," her melancholic gaze, avoiding any eye contact, focused on the distance. My mother confessed to me many years later that at that moment she felt really sorry for *Die Alte*. She would have liked to take her in her arms, but she did not have that intimacy as a daughter-in-law. A little while later my mother discovered a black-and-white photograph of a strange young man stuck in the frame of her mirror. She knew this could only be Jean, the Frenchman.

Once again, my grandmother had succumbed to an unrealistic, romantic illusion. He was in his late 30s, she was in her late 60s – the nice young man with his newly won freedom no longer wanted to know his prison-camp friend, for whom he no longer had room in his life. But the photo remained in the mirror frame.

A reunion of the Schönberg family in 1957, Luisella is second from the left.

In my grandmother's footsteps

*Only those who have scaled the mountain's
highest peak can see into the farthest distance*

❈

My grandmother would have rushed jubilantly into the streets when the Iron Curtain fell in the autumn of 1989, because she had experienced with her own body how life under Communism worked. She was one of the millions of victims of that time. With her story of the *Maskirovka* in the labour camp, she had encapsulated all: dirt was swept under the carpet, making everything appear fine, while the reality was a mess. She said immediately after her return, "Communism is nonsense, it cannot survive in the long run."

Thanks to Google Earth, I was able to take a look at Solikamsky, my grandmother's former labour camp in the Urals, which confirmed my low expectations. With Russia open to the world, I could apply for a visa and just go, which on the one hand would interest me – but what is there still to see? And how complicated is it to get there – just to see a place with huge semi-harvested fields, neglected pavements, decayed buildings, half-starved cattle, straying dogs and a few poor peasants? The brutalities of the Gulags have been recorded, but once no longer in use, they simply disappeared. No monuments were erected, as they were at some of the concentration camps. The shameful and ugly past of World War II wanted to be erased. The Gulags became dots on the map, part of history, which nobody really wanted to remember. Consequently, I have dropped the idea of travelling to the Urals. Just recently I discovered that some of the Gulags made it on the list of tourist attractions.

On the other hand, with my Austrian passport, I could travel to Čonak without even needing a visa because the Ukraine declared its independence from the Soviet Union in August 1991. This seemed like a golden opportunity and as soon as I had solved the problem of how to find my way to Čonak, I decided to go. All the old photographs, diaries, hunting trophies, a detailed map of the property, the two family tombs, of whose whereabouts I knew only a little, did not help me at all. In the meantime, names, places and landscapes had changed. Even the fact that my bedroom in Vienna was a mini-Čonak, with a bear skin hanging over my bed and a wolf skin blanket on my bed, did not give a clue for the upcoming task.

My parents were not drawn back to the old home after the fall of the Iron Curtain. Too much had been destroyed; it was more tempting to hold on to the wonderful memories, rather than having to deal with disappointments. Any post-war claims for compensation were left untouched. But for me, there were neither expectations nor illusions. I was simply curious and wanted to find the reality behind the names Čonak, Uzhgorod, Munkács and Beregvar. The old neighbourly relations with the Schönborn family brought Karl into my life, a native Ukrainian with an Austrian passport, whose grandfather had been in the service of the Schönborn family. He was the very best person I could have found to organise the journey for us.

I travelled with my husband, who is Irish, and my brother-in-law, who wanted to get to know this corner of the world. So, in June 2007 we flew from London to Budapest, where Karl picked us up with a friend in a brand new white Lexus 4D. At the border, we appreciated Karl's presence for the first time when we saw the endless queues of cars waiting for customs clearance. In half an hour all the formalities had been completed, no questions asked and the border barrier lifted; we were spared many frustrating hours. In no time we arrived at our destination, Munkács, which is only 40 kilometres beyond the Hungarian border.

Being so close, I could fully understand that it was no coincidence that the Hungarians ruled here for 600 years, until, after a fierce battle, they had to renounce their territory to the Austrian Habsburg dynasty in 1711. The then emperor, Charles II, handed the domain of Munkács to Bishop Friedrich Karl von Schönborn, as a gesture of good will and gratitude. As he was without any offspring, the entire estate fell to the Austrian line of the Schönborn family in 1746. They brought many Austrian and German settlers to the area, which resulted in an economic boom. It took another hundred years before my ancestors came to this region and our families became great friends.

We stayed in the centre of town, in the best hotel, which was formerly called 'Chilla', and was part of the Schönborns' estates. Now it is called the Star Hotel and belongs to an oligarch who lives in New York. The comfort was limited, the rudeness rather less so. The prices were in line with those of a luxury hotel in Vienna. The building was painted deep yellow, like the beautiful old palace next door, now the Library and Cultural Centre of the town. With the old Schönborn family crest over the entrance portal, it was easy to guess who had built this palace.

I had imagined Munkács, now called Mukachevo, to be a small village similar to Werfen. I was not prepared for a town with a population of 80,000. I imagined dirt roads and horse-drawn carts, stray dogs, and squatters on the side of the road. How wrong I was! Instead, we found a beautiful clean city with a splendid town hall, asphalted pedestrian zones, trees, benches, many coffee houses, modern shops and even a casino. And wherever we looked, so many young people.

Our first goal was to visit Palanok Castle, which sits on a 68-metre high rock towering over the city, and is visible from afar. Its origin dates back to the Middle Ages, it covers an area of 14,000 square metres and boasts

Aerial view of Palanok Castle, Mukachevo (formerly Munkács), Ukraine.

My mother's jacket on display at the folk museum in Palanok Castle.

130 rooms. Here, between 1703 and 1711, under the Hungarian Prince Ferenc Rákóczi II, the national struggle for liberation took place, which was lost to the Habsburgs. After the defeat, the castle was used as a prison from 1798 to 1926, then as military barracks, later as an agricultural college and now as a local museum and gallery. I heard of an oligarch's plan to transform it into a luxury hotel.

Amongst the many Ukrainian visitors, we were the only foreign tourists. The castle seemed to be a popular Sunday destination for young and old. On this beautiful Sunday, even the car park was packed. Newly married couples were having their wedding photos taken at the many dramatic viewing points.

Purposefully, we headed straight for the local folk museum. There was a special reason for this: my parents had decided to donate all the embroidered cushions and blankets which they had saved from Čonak throughout the War years. The present Countess Schönborn, who had resumed strong ties with the new regime, had taken it upon herself to deliver our 'treasures' to the responsible authorities. Naturally, I was dying to see our family possessions again.

Right by the entrance, I came across a huge brown stuffed bear with a raised paw and a missing tooth. I knew from his posture and his missing tooth that he could only have come from Čonak. Once upon a time he had stood tall in my grandfather's study. How did he get here, given that his fate lay in the hands of Russian soldiers, after they had ousted my grandmother from Čonak? Was it out of awe or respect for the big bear that they did not hack him to pieces, as was their custom with most 'useless' items. The inscription beneath said: 'Carpathian bear'.

A few steps further on I tugged Karl excitedly by the sleeve as I discovered the traditional thick, blue-and-white embroidered heavy wool jacket, which my mother often wore when we were still living in Tenneck. With a chamois leather skirt, it was her country-style look; with her masculine haircut, known as an Eton-crop, she was simply not the type for a *Dirndl*, the traditional Austrian dress. The jacket hung crookedly on a wooden hanger; I could not stop myself from straightening it, but nobody restrained me. Close up, I could smell the familiar mothballs.

Then my eyes darted into a room where many colourful embroidered cushions lay on a couch, creating a cosy corner. I immediately recognised all our old cushions, which had decorated my parents' bed for all those years. They were beautifully hand stitched with thin woollen red thread, in symmetrical patterns. I looked at them now with different eyes.

The embroidered white blanket on the couch had been used as a tablecloth at home in Tenneck, and the old tea stain, for which I was to blame, brought back a guilty conscience. I had sweaty hands and unbuttoned my jacket. As though we were total strangers who knew nothing, we admired what used to be ours: I wanted to shout to the young couple who had just passed by hand in hand, "Look, this is from my home, from my parents!" On the small wooden sign was written 'Rusnak hand embroidery'.

A few years ago, according to Countess Schönborn, it had said 'Hand embroidery from the Ditfurth family'. Apparently, such personal

Local handicrafts donated by our family.

acknowledgments are no longer politically correct. Our name had been erased forever. Nevertheless, I was glad that we were able to make a small contribution to the preservation of the local culture, which my family had admired and loved for over four generations. Have any of those skills been preserved?

On our way out, we walked past several rooms which housed a modern-glass exhibition from New York. I imagine that the Star Hotel oligarch had something to do with that. We did not pay much attention to it, as we were absorbed by the past.

After this emotional visit to the museum, we drove to Beregvar to see the Schönborns' old hunting castle. Since the purchase of Čonak, they had been our closest and dearest neighbours (today I am still friends with my generation of the family). In the past, many visits were paid to each other's properties, with the common interests of hunting, gardening, exchanging recipes, playing bridge and of course sharing gossip.

The castle looked just as I remembered it from pictures in the parental photo albums. Built in the neo-Renaissance style, it represents the astrological year: it has 365 windows, 52 rooms and 12 entrances. On the four towers were weathervanes engraved with the year 1890. The clock tower was dominated by the Schönborn coat of arms, the lion. The castle had been perfectly situated in 19 hectares of wonderful natural park land without sacrificing a single oak or fir tree for construction; it was off the road and elevated, like Čonak, which is the only comparison I dare to make. It was indeed a grand family home, and a place 'to die for' – not like Čonak.

Thanks to Karl, we were able to gain entrance to the castle: only a few things, such as the lion's head carved into the wooden staircase, a huge chandelier made of deer antlers and a few wood-panelled rooms, were testimony to a past splendour. In the castle grounds, which resembled an English park, we admired the artificial pond, which was made in the shape of the old Austro-Hungarian Empire to honour the Habsburgs. There, unmistakably, was the famous rose garden, which my grandmother had tried to copy in Čonak without great success. During reciprocal visits, the ladies had always inspected their respective rose gardens.

By now we had almost given in to the illusion that everything here was as it used to be, until two ugly four-storey grey concrete blocks appeared, hidden behind huge old trees. After the expropriation, the property had officially been opened by Khrushchev in 1958 as *Sanatorium Karpaty* and declared a rehabilitation centre for miners and patients with pulmonary diseases. These now dilapidated buildings brought us back to reality.

We left Beregvar behind us and drove down the road to look for another past family jewel – the Schönborn brewery. My father often raved about the Schönborn beer. Karl drove slowly past the old brewery, a row of ghostly buildings where the wind whistled through the roofless halls, with the huge rusty boilers bearing testimony to its past. I wondered how the Schönborns felt about it. Not much further down the road, we came across a factory that appeared in good shape: these were the buildings of the Fischer ski factory. Mr Fischer, a pioneer in making skis, invested in the Ukraine because the labour cost was lower than in Austria. I was surprised that no advertising was displayed on the buildings. A well-known brand would show off that it is not all destruction but investment in the future.

Beregvar, the Schönborns' old hunting castle.

In Čonak at last

*He who repays wickedness with kindness
pours boiling water onto the snow*

❉

As we drove towards Čonak in the pouring rain on a road full of potholes, I was completely immersed in the moment and spoke not a word. I wanted to take in every metre, every stretch of road, because in my thoughts I had gone back a century, imagining sitting in the horse-drawn carriage with my grandmother. The 30 or so kilometres from Munkács to Čonak had taken her a whole day. In the old days they had to negotiate the Litschau Pass, particularly dangerous in winter. At some stage this mountain pass had been 'decapitated' by the Russians, for strategic reasons, now just a flat stretch of road. The small villages with the single-storey houses and their small front gardens reminded me of Burgenland, Austria.

At last, we approached Čonak. The rain eased off a bit and a plateau rose suddenly from the plains. There was a small sign, which I could not read, which said Čonak in Cyrillic, and Karl remarked, "This is the way up to Čonak." Now my heart was beating faster; automatically, I moved closer to the windscreen. That was a moment I will

The turn off to Čonak.

never forget – I was finally at Čonak! The driveway was just as my parents had described it: tall chestnut trees flanked the path, which lent a certain air of prosperity. After a sharp left turn a small parking area appeared, with a barrier blocking the road beyond. As we got out of the car, we immediately felt that the air was fresher and more pleasant. Curiously, we peered through the many trees and discovered a huge meadow stretching out into the distance.

Čonak is the word for barge in Hungarian, and I imagine that this plateau, like a barge, emerged millions of years ago through a dramatic movement of the Earth.

We got out of the car and started exploring: next to a big empty space was an old single-storey house, which could have been the administration house during my grandmother's reign. We entered, and were greeted by two friendly, chubby nurses in clean uniforms. Proudly, they showed us the simple rooms with cracked brown linoleum floors and furniture from the 60s, where Russian children suffering from tuberculosis are brought to convalesce during summer. Although the beds were made up, it gave the impression that no children were expected any longer. Because summer was over, or the 'sanatorium' was no longer in use? We could not find out. The nurses were visibly pleased with our visit because it brought some welcome variety into their monotonous day and they chatted excitedly with Karl. I wish I could have understood what they were saying. Paid by the Russian State, but without any tasks, cleaning seemed their best pastime: the house was incredibly tidy, and the immaculately polished vinyl floors left a lasting impression.

From there we walked down a narrow path and passed a three-storey, uninhabited concrete block with broken windowpanes. Horrified, we looked at this terrible monster. How many years had it been like this? Just a few steps further on, the trees opened out into a square meadow the size of a soccer field only to reveal another huge grey concrete monster. Somewhere there, the one-storey homestead of which I have a picture, had to have been located. I know that soon after the ousting of my grandmother by the Russians, the main house had been razed to the ground, as had the kitchen house, the barn and other outhouses. In their place, two multi-storey 50s-style concrete blocks 'rose from the ashes'. One of these had broken windows and rattling doors, giving rise to the ghastly feeling of total neglect. Only one house, a bit smaller than the other two, seemed habitable. It was built on the best spot, which made me think that it was built on the ruins of our family home. My grandmother, always pragmatic and modern, thought it logical that the Russians should tear down the old family houses, which were impractical for any purpose other than living in. But she was utterly devastated when the 100-year-old oak tree, which had claimed the place of honour in the grounds, was ruthlessly chopped up for firewood. I was pleasantly surprised to see two large oak trees standing proud: one was planted in April 1941 to mark my brother's birth and the other in 1943 to mark my birth. With grandmother's love for nature, this was her way of acknowledging the birth of her grandchildren. "When they are old enough to visit me, they will be impressed to see these beautiful trees," she had said optimistically when she was still the *Panika* in Čonak. She could not have guessed that half a century later I would come to Čonak and did indeed admire the two oaks, mine clearly being a bit smaller than my brother's. It was lucky that these two healthy oaks were not in the way of constructing a further concrete block.

Curiously, next to one of them an ambulance was parked, seemingly from the fifties – I have not seen an old-fashioned ambulance like that since my childhood and wondered if it could still be used.

Surprisingly, we spotted a few men sitting on a bench in front of the only habitable house. Who were they? Workers, ambulance drivers, male nurses, security men? We exchanged curious and suspicious glances. Karl made no attempt to approach them because he wanted to avoid questions. As he had discovered Emma's grave on his reconnaissance trip a few months previously, he hoped to find it again. We passed the men without acknowledgement, looking the other way, but felt their eyes following us.

As I slid down the narrow muddy track behind Karl, my senses on high alert, I worked out that this must have been 'the shouting lane' under Emma's reign of terror – Emma, who's grave we were now heading towards. I glanced back up the track – yes, this narrow passage had been cut out of the woods and there was no doubt about it now. The totally neglected stable buildings at the bottom of the track confirmed my thoughts, being the target of her shouted orders. I wondered, if the daily instructions from all that distance up on the hill really carried that far, especially in wind and rain.

Lost in thought, we kept sliding in the mud along the bumpy path until we reached a small stream. "Of course, it can only be the Poljanski." The story was often told by my grandmother: "We always wanted to build a bridge over it, but each time we got close to it, the prepared timber was stolen the night before work was starting. One day we had had enough. The bridge was never built, and we either balanced on logs or got our feet wet, which was not the end of the world."

But now we walked over a solid wooden bridge, which could be used by trucks transporting timber. It was clear that major deforestation had been taking place over many years. The Russians very quickly discovered the riches of the forest, which they converted into *roubles*. We crossed the bridge and walked along the stream. Karl stopped frequently, looked in all directions, shook his head, went on and stopped, until he stood helpless on one spot. "I'm sorry, but I can no longer find the grave, I'll have to ask one of the men – they'll know for sure." We did not have to go back to the

The house in Čonak in 2007 with the two trees Luisella planted at the birth of her grandchildren.

Standing at the grave of my great grandmother, Emma.

house because one of the men had followed us at a reasonable distance and was immediately helpful. After about 10 minutes trudging further across soggy mossy ground along the stream, he led us uphill into the forest. It seemed endless to me, until suddenly we were standing between the ancient half-dead firs and oaks in front of Emma's grave. Automatically, I folded my hands and stood still.

Such a lonely, deserted, but still dignified grave. The smell of rotten trees intensified thoughts of death. We were all silent. Under the simple cross the old-fashioned cursive script was still clearly legible on the elegantly shaped tombstone:

Emma von Schönberg
geb. Osterrieth
geb. Frankfurt am Main,
25. XI. 1862
gest. Čonak, 30. VI. 1928

As a 66-year-old, the then *Panika*, the lady of the manor, had committed suicide by taking Veronal, the preferred poison at the time.

The year of her death, 1928, can also be regarded as the year the Ukraine died. It was the beginning of the Stalinist era, when 96 per cent of the country was still privately owned. When Stalin, six years earlier, had transformed Russia into the Soviet Union, he had had great plans for the party and for himself as Head of State: the nationalisation of agriculture and the industrialisation of the Ukraine, which had devastating consequences. In the year 1932-1933 the *Politbüro*, with its corrupt and inefficient bureaucracy, insisting on industrialisation, had deported, killed or starved millions of peasants. Luckily the small farmers around Čonak were spared; the property remained within the Schönberg family.

Our new companion asked a lot of questions as he showed us the way to the grave. Of course, he wanted to know how we knew about the grave and why we wanted to visit it. Were we members of the family? No! I had previously agreed with Karl that I was a journalist from England who was documenting the lives of old landowners in the Western Ukraine. Since I spoke English with my husband and brother-in-law, we thought this a most plausible explanation. They could have been historians, producers, directors.

There was a serious reason behind this lie: shortly after the fall of the Iron Curtain, a man in his 40s, who looked like a peasant dressed up in a white shirt, had rung the doorbell of the Ditfurth apartment in Vienna. My mother talked to him through the safety chain of the slightly opened entrance door. In his broken German, he made it clear that he wanted money. It was for four years' accommodation for my grandmother when she was housed in Nikolai's pigsty. He kept repeating the word 'compensation'. My mother, very

Emma's gravestone.

taken aback and frightened, quickly shut the door and sent the stranger away. Then she called a lawyer friend who told her not to pay any money should he come back, because my grandmother had worked for her board and lodging, which was the deal. And besides – who was this stranger? He could have been anybody, even the long arm of the Russian Mafia.

There was no second visit to my mother. Perhaps the man thought that we were too poor because there was no villa, only a simple apartment, no elevator or intercom. There was nothing to suggest money. But my poor mother had the shock of her life.

My mother has since died and my brother no longer lives in Vienna. But just to be on the safe side, I did not want to reveal a family connection.

Before we said good-bye to our curious companion, Karl exchanged mobile numbers with him.

We left Čonak, and were now back on the main road, in search of my grandfather's grave. After a short drive, Karl suddenly stopped at a dirt road: "I think it is this way." We opened our umbrellas and trudged along the dirt road. Again, it seemed to me endlessly long. Half-harvested stalks of corn, carelessly thrown away water bottles which recalled hot summer days, a slow-burning dung heap in the middle of the field – it was as if there was an award for environmental pollution. I imagined my grandmother as a working-woman in a worn-out black dress with a headscarf, digging in these fields for days on end. Here is what she wrote:

"I have got a bit of a field in Kerecky, where I've already grown potatoes and on a piece of field in Bereznik (the bigger one) I have planted corn, beans, cabbage; very country-like and à la Rusnak. One should take these people by the throat on a crash course and teach them how to really do agriculture, but I have come to the conclusion that they do not want to learn and thus I am finished with them. The real Russians understand much more about it. Of forestry one had better not speak; only the Czechs are good at that."

This was part of a letter written in spring 1948.

≈

Although my grandfather Moriz had died seven years after his mother-in-law Emma, his gravestone was broken in half and illegible. My penny-pinching grandmother certainly chose the cheapest stone she could find in Munkács for her husband. She did not care what people would say or think. She chose a plot in a field – nowhere near Emma's grave, but on the opposite side of Čonak. Only the birch tree, which Hermann, the chief gamekeeper had later planted in my grandfather's honour, gave the grave some dignity. In addition, many years later, the local doctor paid for iron railings to surround the plot, which meant that at least the cows could no longer pollute my grandfather's grave.

It crossed my mind that *Die Alte* never mentioned in any of her letters having visited the grave, which was adjacent to one of the fields where she had laboured and hacked away for four years. Was there no spark of love or sentimentality left? No feelings whatsoever? My parents always said, "She never looked back, even in the worst situations," – that was her strength. But in this case, a cold shudder ran down my back.

My mother had told me about the gruesome funeral. It was an ice-cold January day in 1936. My parents, married for less than a year, arrived in record time from Vienna after they had received a telegram with the sad news. My grandmother, the 47-year-old widow, dressed in black and wearing pearls, greeted my parents stony faced. Without any explanation, she said to my father, "Just so you know, Franzl, I don't want you to cry." She set a good example by showing no emotion at all. There were candles everywhere and fresh-smelling branches of fir framed the wooden coffin, which had been set up in my grandfather's study. The lid was still open,

My grandfather, Moriz's grave – then and now.

so that my father and the staff could say good-bye face-to-face. *Haifa*, the cook, sobbed uncontrollably; Pepi was drowning in tears. The hunters took it in turns to stand guard by the coffin, struggling with their composure. There was great sadness all around. My grandmother, the 'Master of Ceremonies', showed no emotion at all (she had probably lost any feelings for her husband a long time ago). She explained to my mother, "As a lady, you must be in control, know how to behave, never show your feelings, just like the English Royal Family, who are my role models." And so my mother did not dare to shed a tear either.

The following day, a convoy of horse-drawn carriages, the first one carrying the closed coffin, drove over the desolate field and across the small, frozen stream to a slightly sloping meadow that offered a magnificent view back towards Čonak.

No location had been designated and with a great deal of effort a hole was dug at random in the frozen soil with picks and shovels. It was as if nature was resisting. An icy wind blew over the fields, carrying the weeping and sobbing voices of the women far into the distance. When my 24-year-old father could no longer hold back his tears, he was sharply reprimanded by his mother, "Stop crying!" My young parents huddled very close together, giving each other warmth and protection. My mother was so afraid of this new mother-in-law that her blood froze in her veins. With all her strength, she suppressed the tears that welled up inside her. It was no surprise that my mother's voice started to tremble when she recounted the funeral.

The next day, very early in the morning, my parents jumped into their car and left Čonak in a great hurry. Was this unworthy tomb my grandmother's final revenge on her husband and the Ditfurth family? Should I stop wasting any compassion on my grandmother right now?

Karl's cell phone rang. The curious man from the visit to Čonak had a question: would we like to drive to Bereznik and visit the house where the Baroness had lived for four years? Into the lions' den! Karl looked at me questioningly. I nodded. My heart stopped for a second. Despite some reservations, the curiosity overwhelmed me. What a unique opportunity to see how *Die Alte* had lived as a farmer's maid for four years. In my wildest dreams, I could not have imagined that I would actually come so close to her past. Now it was getting exciting beyond belief.

At the second attempt, Karl found House No.4 in Bereznik. Familiar with the address written on her many letters, it never ever occurred to me that I might ever actually be in the place where I could still feel *Die Alte's* presence. My trip to the Ukraine had turned out to be much more valuable than a visit to the demolished Gulag in the Urals could ever have been.

When we got out of the car, our feet sank deep into the mud. We could hear the grunting of the pigs from the barn. Yes, that's how I imagined it. A small house with only two rooms, cleaner than expected, and very simple. A woman in her 40s greeted us and asked us to leave our shoes outside the house. Karl thought she could be the curious man's wife. She was a schoolteacher. She asked Karl sharply, "Where do you come from, what do you want?" Karl gave her the journalist story. She led us into a room that was a kitchen, dining room and bedroom all in one. A toothless old woman dressed in black, wearing the customary headscarf – she looked like my grandmother when she had returned from Russia – was waiting in the kitchen and immediately broke into a torrent of words over the Baronesa. Her gestures showed great excitement. I kept a poker face while I listened and took in every detail of the room. The schoolteacher served us very good black coffee. Karl translated from Ukrainian into German, I translated into English. I kept up the pretence when, from under the bed, an old shoe box was produced with many Ditfurth family photographs. Most of them I had seen in our albums. They were probably copies which my grandmother had quickly gathered up when she was thrown out of Čonak.

The chatty old woman was interrupted again and again by the teacher (her daughter?) saying that she was quite senile and had gone crazy, haunted by a ghost. "The Baronesa appeared to her as a ghost, because she could not find peace until she had a handful of soil from Čonak on her grave. She raised both arms, her eyes directed towards the sky, and gave a deep sigh, repeating herself. Someone from the family must come to save her from this curse." Was that 'someone' directed at me?

After a quick calculation, I realised that she was the schoolgirl from whom my grandmother had borrowed pen and ink and writing paper, torn out of her exercise books. I deliberately pretended not to be very interested.

Then came the bombshell from the teacher, via Karl's translation: the Baronesa had had twins in her second marriage, two girls, one of them lives in Australia. Clearly, this was aimed at me. My poker face remained intact. I pretended to be amazed, but not shocked, and did not explain that such a thing was totally impossible.

When my grandmother had married for the second time, she was 47 years old. Did she seem much younger to the locals, who aged prematurely because of their hard work? She was already in her 50s when she joined the Nikolai household. How come the schoolteacher had heard about Australia? The only explanation I have is gossip through the Schönborn connection.

Karl probed no further. The teacher started to become slightly agitated because the old woman was not to be stopped but pulled a blanket from the bed in the kitchen, which she held to my face: "It is a blanket from the Baronesa," she announced with pride; she had been sleeping under it ever since she had 'disappeared'. Self-control was needed since I would have liked to hold it against me briefly, just to feel it, to smell it.

All of a sudden the mood changed: the schoolteacher became business-like. It was only recently that Ukrainian television had been at their place making a documentary about former landowners. If we wanted to know more, then we should inquire there. She did not want to waste any more time with us. She had cast all her bait without catching a fish. Karl nodded, knowingly. It was clear that from now on no further information would be available without a 'donation'. A giant antler hung above the entrance door. "We are waiting for someone from the family to come and pick it up," the toothless old woman mumbled. One last bait. I quickly looked at it, shrugged my shoulders in a 'What can I do?' gesture and slipped back into my dirty shoes. On the way out I cast a last glance at the pigsty. Too bad I had no excuse to look in there.

I was dying to pull out my camera but knew that this was a total "no-no".

How different would our visit have been if I had told them that I was the Baronesa's granddaughter? The toothless woman would have sobbed, talking even more incomprehensibly. Would she have taken me into her arms? The schoolteacher would have wondered how much money she could extract – I think.

On our drive back to Munkács, Karl and I discussed all the possible variations of our visit. Did they believe our cover story? How did Australia and the twins come into play?

The next day, Karl accompanied us back to Budapest. How can I ever thank him for this unforgettable journey back to my ancestors?

Lungau

A man attends to his hair on a daily basis, why not to his heart?

After a couple of weeks of family life, the moment had come when my father, without any thoughts of revenge, said to *Die Alte* after supper: "You can stay here for three months, but then you have to look for a new home," which she took with good grace. Perhaps she had already had enough of family life and longed for independence.

Not only was our apartment too small in the long run, with the five of us having to share one bath and one lavatory, but also my grandmother had begun to interfere more and more in all areas of everyday life: "Oh, *Kindchen*, not like that," still rings in my ears today. Our old cook, Steffi, became more hysterical than ever, her stuttered words even more incomprehensible. The four of us, as a family unit, were disrupted in our rhythm of life. My father, now in his mid-40s, did not suddenly want to be dominated by his mother again. My parents had a harmonious marriage and we had a happy family life. Sport was very important to us. We were a good team of four when it came to tennis, ping-pong or bridge. In the summer we went hiking in the mountains, in the winter we went skiing. How was *Die Alte* to fill her time with us? Besides there was no room for a fifth person in our Jeep.

There would have been a few old friends in Vienna who might have received her in their homes, but the transition from the Russian labour camp to the big city might have been too great a step. In her heart of hearts, *Die Alte* was a country girl. And yet, in spite of all the hardships she had gone through, she never ceased to be a lady, so the environment for her new life needed to have some style and dignity.

She, too, had been thinking about her future, and together an ideal solution was found. She could move in with her childhood friend Joli, by now a confirmed spinster. The parents of both women had shared magnificent hunting grounds before World War I in the district of Lungau, where Joli still lived. They had spent many summers there as children during the years when Čonak was made unsafe by the Partisans. My father, as a 12-year-old, shot his first chamois there. The nearby fortress of Finstergrün in Ramingstein belonged to Joli, officially known as the Countess Jolanta Szápáry, called *Tante* Joli by us children. In almost every letter from the Carpathians, Joli was sent greetings by *Die Alte*. Sometimes there were some cutting remarks, sometimes specific questions, but Joli was never forgotten.

Joli lived in a typical wooden Austrian country house next to the fortress. As the upkeep of the fortress consumed more money than Joli had, she was very happy at the idea of having her old childhood friend, Luisella, move into her house as a paying guest, which seemed a wonderful solution to everybody. Everything about it was positive: the low cost of living in the country, the familiarity of the environment, the old friendship and the relative proximity to us. Joli had a small staff and maintained a modest but dignified household.

It was about three hours by car from Tenneck, over the Tauern Pass, which always posed a challenge during the winter months because of its steep and narrow road. As it turned out, *Die Alte*, very appropriately, was now going to live in the coldest region in Austria.

For the last time we squeezed into our Jeep again when we drove over the Tauern Pass to the Lungau, not knowing that there would be a huge reward at the end of this trip: the Finstergrün fortress was every child's dream. We had never had the opportunity to run around in a real half-ruined castle, playing 'cops and robbers' and exploring empty towers and dark, scary caves. I envied my grandmother her new home and would have liked to stay there forever.

Religion was never a high priority in our family, so *Tante* Joli's deep faith was a whole new experience for us. In an overwhelmingly Catholic country, my brother and I, as Protestants, were excluded from religious education at school. We did not feel ostracised in any way but enjoyed a free hour. *Tante* Joli showed us what the Catholic faith really meant to her: she said the Lord's Prayer before every meal, went to church, confession and communion every Sunday and on religious holidays, and made the sign of the cross on our foreheads every time she said hello or good-bye to us, murmuring short blessings. Like all Catholics of her time and status, she had an oil painting of the Virgin Mary hanging over her bed. When we went for a walk and passed a wayside chapel, she crossed herself. My grandmother tolerated her faith and remarked again: "Some people have religion, some people need religion." So Joli practised her religion without being criticised by *Die Alte*. For harmony's sake, Joli tolerated my grandmother's smoking without a word.

Christmas 1955 was the first with *Die Alte* as a free person which we spent altogether in the cosy house of *Tante* Joli. There was much praying and singing, rather than gifts, which were sparse in those days. Living with Joli seemed harmonious. They had a lot to talk about, there were enough common acquaintances, many childhood memories were exchanged,

The town of Ramingstein in Austria, with the fortress of Finstergrün overlooking the town.

politics were discussed, and every now and then gossip provided more conversation. Reading and playing cards shortened the evenings. My grandmother showed her great sense of humour when Joli drove her old VW Beetle and sat so far forward that the vehicle's horn always hooted when she braked hard.

After the second summer, the idyll in the cosy house came to an end: "We've agreed to separate." It sounded like an amicable divorce. The real 'grounds for divorce' were flowers: the watering of the pelargoniums. As a passionate gardener, Joli had not just a magnificent garden, but also wonderful red pelargoniums in all the windows of her house. My grandmother was always trying to tell her how to do it better or differently, until one day the good-natured Joli lost her patience – after all, they were her flowers in her house.

Die Alte, quietly frustrated at not getting things done her way, simply collected her few possessions and moved to the nearby town of Tamsweg, where she rented a small apartment in the attic of the Pension Waldmann, in the centre of town. Naturally, she remained friends with Joli. This was the first time ever that she would have to take care of herself without supporting staff, controlling peasants or prison guards. Born in 1888 when radio, telephone, television and cars did not exist, she adapted easily to all things modern, embracing them with great enthusiasm. She learned to cook and bought a vacuum cleaner: "A really practical thing," she remarked.

The new apartment was comfortably furnished in the traditional way of the Lungau. Instead of Rusnak blankets there were now Lungauer blankets, locally made rugs instead of kilims, and cushions with local embroidery. The only thing missing were hunting trophies, such as deer antlers, a wild boar's head, fox furs and bear skins, to bring back the atmosphere of Čonak. Silver cutlery was no longer a must, the familiar *Gmundner* ceramics came with a new design. With the traditional tiled stove in the corner of the living room giving out a steady heat, heavy old wooden beams supporting the low ceiling, creaking floorboards making a pleasant sound, and the smell of wood, all added up to make my grandmother feel perfectly at home. She became known as 'the Baroness from Tamsweg' or 'Die Sacher'. There was no need for a guest room because her guests, like us, could be accommodated in the Pension Waldmann. Since she was a bookworm, the empty bookshelves quickly filled up with reading material in three languages. She read *Die Presse* every day and subscribed to *Paris Match* and *Time Magazine*. She followed the stock market, gathered information about everything and turned her energy and attention to the future.

≈

On 18th May, 1958, in the best hotel of Salzburg, Österreichischer Hof, we celebrated my grandmother's 70th birthday with lunch in an elegant private room.

At the time, she used lipstick, concealed her brown age spots with makeup, powdered her nose and brushed rouge onto her cheeks. She no longer used Chanel N°5. Uncle Wolf came with his wife and the customary bottle of champagne. Because tradition and good manners required it, my mother insisted that my father make a speech. My father, who absolutely did not want to do this because of his ambivalent feelings towards his mother, was very reluctant, but was forced to conform and fulfil his duty as a son.

After the main course, which was *Wiener Schnitzel*, our favourite dish, he tapped his champagne glass, stood up and in a completely flat tone started to speak. No notes. It turned out to be the most embarrassing speech of his life: "…So you are still with us, and here you are again, which we did not expect…" – more an accusation than a celebration of life. Totally devoid of joy.

In order to avoid eye contact, we just stared into our plates. My mother gave me a nudge under the table. No one dared to look at *Die Alte* during the speech. Like all bad speeches, it was too long, and when my father realised that he had not found the right tone, he kept on talking. When he finally sat down embarrassed silence followed, until Uncle Wolf saved the occasion with "Once again – long live Luisella!"

My father could never forgive her for marrying Herr Sacher.

In that same year, our family itself was in turmoil: my father's job in Tenneck had come to an end after 12 years and with a heavy heart we had relocated to Salzburg. My father hated his new job, and my brother and I had problems settling into new high schools. I had broken both legs in the last ski race of the season and limped with both legs in plaster into the Österreichischer Hof. It was well and truly our *Annus horribilis* (a very bad year). Fortunately, a year later my father found his dream job in Vienna, which meant that the car trip to the Lungau now took a full day and mutual visits were limited to festive events. Once again, communication was conducted by letter.

But now we were much closer to my other grandmother, who lived near Vienna. She was the 'fairy-tale grandmother', with lots of cuddles and chocolate biscuits, loving words and no fear.

Die Alte came to Vienna on important occasions, such as high school graduations, or on special birthdays. During these visits she stayed with us, always expressed her opinion, criticised every family member near and far, even those who were just leaving the room. Only about my mother did she never say a bad word. As an 18-year-old, I thought to myself that the nickname 'Witch of the Urals' was well chosen.

She went on two last great journeys in her life. The first took her to Düsseldorf to visit her missing husband's mother and sister. What did they think of this unconventional marriage? Did she want to find closure through her visit or was she secretly hoping to find him there? Sixteen years had passed since Georg Sacher had disappeared without a trace and she was still searching for him. It must have been undying love.

Her second major journey took her to Istanbul, which had been the largest city in Europe during the Middle Ages. Its history had always fascinated her; she had read so much about it and needed to satisfy her curiosity. Was the strong attraction of Central Asia a coincidence or an inherited gene from her grandfather, Wolf Erich?

Despite her 'war-widow's pension' which she received from Germany because of her missing husband, and the 'late-returnee pension' which she got from Austria, plus the small remnants of her former wealth, she travelled quite modestly with a tour group by coach. She would rarely take a taxi.

Only once did she splash out on a little luxury and bought a TV set, because she wanted to witness live the first man landing on the moon on 21st July, 1969. Ever since her childhood, the moon had held her fascination. Children's books and the wolves of Čonak were to blame.

Always practical in her approach to things, getting older and living in an attic without a lift was no problem for her. On the principal of never being dependent on the kindness of other people, she organised a whole 'army' of schoolchildren who willingly, for a few *schillings* pocket money, went shopping for her, brought her *Die Presse* every morning before school, and ran other errands.

When cooking became too laborious, the employees of the Pension Waldmann brought her meals upstairs. The nurses from the hospital in Tamsweg also came whenever she needed help. She was popular with everybody because she never wanted to take advantage of people, honoured every favour, never complained and was never bad-tempered. Everybody was happy to help her.

Six months before her death, I saw my grandmother for the last time. I was 27 years old and drove alone from Vienna, which took me the best part of a day. I did it out of duty.

She never mentioned her illness to me, because: "In such things, young people have no interest anyway." She never talked about Russia, her childhood or her experiences in life, as a result of which the evening was hard work, confined to family gossip and superficial conversation. What a shame – I am thinking now. In order to lighten this evening of duty, I decided to buy a bottle of red wine and hoped my grandmother would share it with me. Sadly, she did not, which meant that I probably drank most of the bottle.

In her eyes, I was likely seen as a failure – I had graduated from high school but did not get a university degree, and there was no man in sight to marry. I also felt like a failure myself: my career as a ski racer had ended without the dreamed-of Olympic medal. I spent the summer months in Australia as a ski instructor, which was not considered a proper profession within the family. Back in Austria, I worked as a freelance employee for *Tyrolia* ski bindings – again, not considered a serious job. My brother, on the other hand, had now become a Doctor of Jurisprudence and a state official in the Treasury.

After this stilted evening and a good night's sleep, thanks to the red wine, I drove back to Vienna. Immediately, *Die Alte* wrote a letter to my mother:

"I have to tell you in confidence that Chrissi is an alcoholic which you already see in her swollen hands."

This stab in the back left a bitter taste for me.

Death

*The wolf does not lose its dignity
even in its fight with death*

❋

"I have to tell you something unpleasant." With these words, *Die Alte* informed my mother that she had cancer. The fact that cancer had now taken up residence in her body – the superwoman, who had survived Russia for 10 years without any illness – annoyed her immensely. As an 80-year-old woman, she still felt strong and healthy, so how dare her body suddenly let her down. Did breast cancer have anything to do with smoking? "Nonsense, it has nothing to do with it," as she knew better than anyone. Since the first operation, when both breasts were removed, two years had passed. "Well, that's how it is." She accepted her condition in a fatalistic fashion. Of course, feeling sorry for herself was not in her nature.

But thoughts of suicide seemed to swirl around her head. "I could kill myself," she mentioned casually in conversation with my mother. Maybe she was thinking of Emma, her mother, who had decided when and where she wanted to die. Was it about her not wanting to give up control over her life? During one of the hospital visits, she gave my mother a handful of tablets: "Keep those please." Having no idea what sort of tablets they were, my mother remembered the talk of suicide and felt most uncomfortable because she thought these could be the tablets for later.

Because phone calls to Vienna were regarded as much too expensive, even during her illness she still only corresponded through letters. A few months after we saw her, a letter came from Salzburg, which meant that *Die Alte* must be in hospital again.

> "The cancer has again become annoying; my doctor, Dr Lainer, has insisted that I go into hospital."

Immediately my mother realised that she had to get in the car. Although my grandmother could easily have afforded it, she remained in the public ward and did not seek specialist treatment: "Look, it is perfectly all right to share a room with other people – who needs anything more."

My father, who was still working, did not consider taking leave to visit her in hospital; besides, he deemed such visits a matter for women. He did not suddenly become sentimental or have a late surge of yearning for motherly love or find the need to forgive and be reconciled. "I do not regret anything and went my own way," she had said immediately after her return, which was now 15 years back. Everything had been said then and what was not said, but swept under the carpet, was to remain there.

When my mother entered the large, musty hospital room, she realised the gravity of the situation as soon as she saw her mother-in-law's sunken, hollow eyes, which already seemed more empty than alive. After a weak embrace, *Die Alte* opened her bedside table and handed over another handful of pills to my mother: "Please throw them away before the nurses find them, they won't help anymore, it's all nonsense, I've had enough of all that stuff." Enduring pain was never a problem; she simply did not see any point in fighting nature any longer. She knew that her time was up. Since she had always compared humans with animals, she clearly felt that nature should be allowed to take its course from now on. Perhaps she was thinking of Chimmy, her beloved Skye Terrier, whom she had shot with her pistol when he could no longer walk.

Her next request was: "Give this to Franzl and tell him that he can take care of everything now." It was a brown envelope with bank statements of the meagre remains of her fortune. No confession, no sentimentality, no tears. The Catholic priest came to her bedside and was told in no uncertain terms: "You do not have to come and see me." Then the topic turned again to the latest gossip about friends and family. When my mother bent down and kissed her good-bye, she knew the end had come. That same night my grandmother died. In her one-page will, she expressed two wishes: that she should be buried in Tamsweg with her wedding ring, and that on her gravestone only 'Luisella Sacher' was to be engraved. This was the ultimate snub to her, our, family.

She certainly did it all her way!

The last photo of Luisella Sacher.

Epilogue: Uninvolved and yet familiar!

(Dr. Helga Leinweber, born Lainer)

Thanks to a very lucky circumstance, I was able to read this book in its first draft. I had no idea who the 'Witch of the Urals' was, who *Die Alte*, the author's grandmother was, but when I saw the photograph of the old lady, a window opened onto my own past.

I was once again the young girl who had grown up in the place under the castle of Finstergrün. Utterly amazed, I turned the pages. After so many years, I would now learn more about this woman who was so mysterious to me at the time. I can't remember how old I was when I saw her for the first time. Eleven? Twelve? Most of my memories are buried in the depths of the past and only a few of them reappeared whilst reading through this book.

Already before World War I, the family of my grandfather, who was then a general practitioner in Ramingstein, and the old Countess Margit Szápáry, the mother of *Tante* Joli (Aunt Joli), had developed an uncomplicated friendship, which passed down to the next generation and to us children. In the small town – just like Tenneck – everyone knew everyone, everyone was appreciated, and we helped each other. There were five telephone connections at that time: in the post office, in the vicarage, in the house of Jolántha Szápáry, in my parents' place (the doctor's surgery) and in the stately Schwarzenberg's forestry administration. The phone rang in that order: if it rang four times, the doctor was required; if it rang five times, my father heaved a sigh of relief – the forestry administration was required. *Tante* Joli only had to give way to the post office and the church.

After graduating from high school in Graz, I worked as an assistant to my father. At that time, *Tante* Joli's rattling orange VW Beetle was often parked in front of our house. She seldom came alone; she usually had a friend or a guest with her. And thus, I saw *Die Alte* suddenly in my memory, sitting at the table of my parents' house. "What I can do, I will do, Baroness". Whether my father said this in so many words I do not know any longer, but he helped her as a doctor as best he could and, when the phone rang four times for the doctor, he sent me with medicines for her up to *Tante* Joli's cosy house where *Tante* Joli often invited me to tea in her wood-panelled dining room. Later I would go to the attic in the Pension Waldmann when the Baroness moved there.

As I reflected on her face and drew a mental picture in my mind, I also remembered a deep, rough voice, solid shoes, and an energetic person – simply a woman who never faded into the background. For me, she was always surrounded by a touch of mystery. My parents certainly knew more about her and about her life, but in front us – or with us – it was never talked about. If only I had known then of the extraordinary events the life of this woman had encompassed, events about which I was only now reading in this book. I also do not recall that the names Ditfurth or Schönberg were ever mentioned in connection with her in my presence, which is why the relationship between the author's grandmother and the 'Witch of the Urals' came as quite a shock when I read this book. For me she was the Baroness Sacher or simply *'Die Sacher'*. Smoking? In my mother's opinion that was not at all suitable for a woman at the time – but the self-confidence with which the Baroness did it, I just found admirable. My father was also a smoker, but at the time I admired this feminine self-assurance very much.

Things that are of interest to me today were only a fleeting reference to my youthful self. The Cosel? Yes, a famous woman. But where had she lived? Somewhere far away from Austria, behind the Iron Curtain, which was off limits for everybody. Three months before I had this book in my hands, I was in Dresden, Pillnitz Castle and Stolpen Castle for the first time, unfortunately without any knowledge of these relationships.

In 1970, when this remarkable woman died, I was teaching in Tamsweg, very close to Pension Waldmann, as a sports instructor at the high school. That she was so seriously ill I did not know. Later I completed my doctorate in sports medicine, married and moved to Hessen, Germany. The traces of my youth were blurred, and I never heard any more about this woman. But she is still alive in the memory of the village because my brother, now himself a doctor in Ramingstein, and even his senior staff still have some knowledge of the Baroness of Tamsweg, as she was remembered.

The author of this book, with whom I spent a few days as a child at the hunting lodge of the Szápáry family, had long since disappeared from my field of vision – until many years later and quite by chance I discovered her book *The World Is My Home*. Of course, I bought it and we got in touch once again.

Many an impression of 'Die Sacher' was revived through her granddaughter's writing. Without any touch of arrogance, always friendly towards my family, and, for me, a little mysterious, 'Die Sacher' has emerged from my memory – a model for women today who try to prove themselves through pointless feminine gestures. Christina's grandmother never needed this. What a shame she cannot tell us more about her extraordinary life.

Notes

Political situation in the Carpatho-Ukraine:
1000–1918: Kingdom of Hungary, Carpatho-Ukraine was part of it
1867–1918: Carpatho-Ukraine became part of the Austro Hungarian Empire
1916–1922: Partisan invasion
1919–1941: Czechoslovakian Administration
1941–1944: German Occupation – 1.4 million people killed
1945: Russian invasion/expropriation of Čonak/now Ukraine
1991: Ukraine declares Independence from the Soviet Union

Čonak's family history:
Wolf Erich (original buyer): mostly absent after purchase in 1859
Donald (his son): inherited Čonak in 1883
Emma (Donald's wife) started her reign: about 1890–1928
Wolf Erich (Emma's son) was born in Čonak, 1895
Emma was forced to leave Čonak in 1918 (Partisan invasion)
Emma's return to Čonak: 1922 – ruled for six more years
Moriz von Ditfurth (Emma's son-in-law) administrator: 1926–1928
Emma dies in Čonak: 1928
Luisella (Emma's daughter) reigned in Čonak: 1928-1945

Family:
1812–1883: Wolf Erich von Schönberg
1833–1857: Luisella Karoline von Kiel (first wife)
1838–1903: Christiana Fiennes-Lumley (second wife)
1854–1926: Donald von Schönberg (his son)
1862–1928: Emma von Osterrieth (Donald's wife)
1888–1970: Luisella von Schönberg (daughter)
1895–1981: Wolf Erich (Uncle Wolf, Luisella's brother)
1873–1935: Moriz von Ditfurth (Luisella's first husband)
1913 – missing in action: Georg Wilhelm Sacher (Luisella's second husband)
1911–1994: Franz Dietrich XV von Ditfurth (Luisella's only child)
1910–2000: Maria Helene von Ditfurth (geb. von Puchberger)
1941– Nikolaus Balthasar Ditfurth
1943– Christina Isabella Ditfurth

The Ditfurth family lived in Vienna until 1941
1941–1945 in Lebring, state of Styria
1945–1957 in Tenneck, state of Salzburg
1957–1958 in Salzburg
1959–2000 in Vienna

Luisella von Schönberg: 1888–1970:
- Grew up in Germany, married and moved to Vienna in 1911
- Lived more or less in Čonak: 1928–1944
- Lived as a maid in the pigsty in Bereznik: 1945–1949
- Went missing from 1949–1955: Gulag in the Ural Mountains
- Released from Gulag: August 1955
- Ramingstein and Tamsweg (Lungau, Austria): 1956–1970
- Died in Salzburg 1970, buried in Tamsweg

Historical events:
1914–1918: World War I
1939–1945: World War II
1933: Adolf Hitler comes to power in Germany
1938: *Anschluss* of Austria, integration into the German Reich
   Night of the Broken Glass – *Kristallnacht* – November
1945–1955: Allied occupation of Austria: partition of Vienna and Austria
   into four allied zones (American, British, French and Russian)
1953: Stalin's death
1955: Austria becomes an independent, neutral state

Footnotes

1. Wolf Erich von Schönberg's painting is from the book:
   Red-green Lions. The von Schönberg family in Saxony, Adel in Sachsen Vol. 4, written by Matthias Donath, Meißen 2014.

2. Wolf Erich von Schönberg wrote: *Travels in India and Kashmir* in two volumes. The book was published in London by Hurst and Blackett, Publishers, Successors to Henry Colburn, in 1853.
   The book is available in the London Library.

3. Quotes on pages 151 and 152 are from a booklet:
   Forced Labour in the Soviet Union (Neue Welt Verlag) Vienna 1953.

Emil & Franzl after a successful hunt.

My parents, Maria and Franzl.

My father with my brother Nikolaus.

Transporting the kill, summer 1942.

My mother the trendsetter.

Čonak trophies in our apartment.

My mother with my brother Nikolaus.

Me and my brother in Tenneck.

Mother on a logging expedition, Čonak.

Father at his first accounting job, 1939.

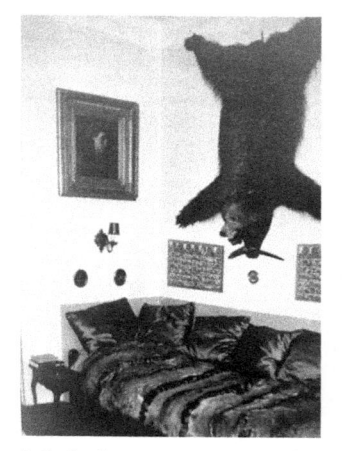

My bedroom in Vienna, bear and wolf skins from Čonak.

Blühnbach Castle.

The Ditfurth family in Vienna, 1965, Christina (the author) top left.

This symbol represents the Edelweiss,
a famous Austrian alpine flower.

About the Author, Christina von Ditfurth

I was born in 1943 in post-war Austria into an impoverished aristocratic family. Through political circumstances we were refugees in our own country, having lost everything.

My brother and I grew up thinking our paternal grandmother had died somewhere in Russia.

We lived in a small village surrounded by high mountains covered in snow. Skiing came naturally to me and I became a member of the Austrian National Ski Team (1961–1967) which opened a window to the world for me. In 1968 I retired from ski racing and came to Australia as a ski instructor for the winter months.

Back in Austria, I started a marketing career in the ski business promoting Tyrolia ski bindings, now known under the famous brand name of HEAD. Eventually my job took me to Japan where we increased the market share dramatically, which earned me the AMF Chairman's Business Award 1983 – the highest award given to a woman.

After 17 years with HEAD, I decided to start my own business – Christina Consulting Japan – which provided me with a number of roles: a Cultural Lecturer for Asahi Shinbum, running Elegance Seminars for ladies, a 'Pin Up Girl' for White Pia Ski resort, and consultant for Hayman Island on the lucrative Japanese market when it reopened in the 1980s.

I published three books in Japan covering lifestyle, business and marriage. I was a Special Correspondent during the Nagano Olympics in 1998 for Shinano Mainichi, the local newspaper, and had a regular column in Ski Graphic.

The most challenging writing experience was as an 'Agony Aunt' for the Japanese Magazine MIL.

I have also written a book about my time as a ski racer: *"The World is my Home"* (*Die Welt ist meine Heimat*) 2006.

Skiing is still my greatest passion and I aim to keep helicopter skiing in Kamchatka, Russia.

I married John L. Stitt in 1993. We live in Sydney and have no children.